MW01169586

Performance Avenues

Knowing How We Work

A new approach to understanding the five avenues we work on every day as leaders, learners, innovators, managers and promoters as well as testing and evaluating our performance type.

Tom Despard

XULON PRESS

© 2002 by Tom Despard

Performance Avenues
by Tom Despard

Printed in the United States of America

Library of Congress Control Number: 2002100983
ISBN 1-931232-98-9

All rights reserved. No part of this publication may be reproduced or transmitted in any form or by any means without written permission of the publisher.

Xulon Press
11350 Random Hills Road
Suite 800
Fairfax, VA 22030
(703) 279-6511
XulonPress.com

Thomas E. Despard
and Despard Associates, LLC
220 Eshelman Road
Lancaster, PA 17601 USA
717-394-7882
Fax: 717-394-7883
E-mail: tdespard@aol.com

Dedication

This book is dedicated to the entrepreneurs in my family
who have gone on before me, transformed their industries
and made my path smoother.

Tom Despard
Lancaster, PA, USA

Contents

Foreword

A fter 30 years in the commercial and residential developing and building business, I decided to write a practical well-researched book that I myself would like to read and to enlighten me and enhance my own performance. *Performance Avenues, Knowing How We Work* is a new approach to understanding the five avenues we work on everyday as leaders, learners, innovators, managers and promoters as well as testing and evaluating our performance type.

What is this New Approach?

For years business books have focused on management psychology, personality types, thinking styles and behavioral patterns. There are many good books on these subjects that are well worth reading. *But what is not currently available is a book that analyzes businessmen and women in terms of their five basic modes of operation—as leaders, learners, innovators, managers, and promoters. We call these **performance avenues**.* For example, there are many books on management, but Manager Avenue is only one of the five ways to reach and stay at one's peak performance in your business endeavors.

After a discussion about evaluating yourself, this book reviews the latest thinking concerning these five performance avenues to refresh the reader with a working knowledge baseline of each avenue. We then take a look at the strengths and weaknesses of the ten *performance types* such as Leader-Promoter, Learner-Innovator, or Promoter-Manager that are defined using a person's two most dominant avenues. These definitions are followed by the Despard Performance Type Test, a one hundred question test that determines an individual's performance type. The reader will be able to type himself and better understand how he functions on the job, how to improve himself, how to relate to others better.

Ask business people what is their greatest asset and most will tell you it's their people. Ask them what their biggest problems are with their people, and they will answer it is understanding them, getting them to perform better and getting the company to synergistically perform better through them. Businesses use all kinds of ways to do this—common sense, experience, personality testing and typing, trial and error, employee manuals, the suggestion box, training and seminars, articles, books and newsletters, enlightened supervision, and motivational tools galore—you name it. A lot of these things work very well, but, as I have observed over many years in business, they are still missing something.

That missing something is understanding how people usually perform everyday in the work environment. Are they leading, learning, innovating, managing, or promoting most of the time—that is, *what is there natural mode of operation in which they are most comfortable and effective?* I'm not concerned for the moment whether they are introverts or extroverts or thinkers or feelers, but rather with which performance avenue they both like best and are best at. I want to be able to understand and predict their behavior. I don't want—and can't afford—to have the wrong person in the wrong job doing the wrong thing. *There's a labor shortage and there will always be a shortage of high performance people available to a business. Businesses must to be more effective with the people they have.*

Hence the concept of the five performance avenues along with the identifying system of performance types. This book is short and direct with the bullets and bytes business people are most likely not only to read, but more importantly, to retain and use. It is a pocket guide to what it is to be a leader, learner, innovator, manager, and promoter. I could have used just such a handy reference many times in my career.

Why Read this Book?

The goal of this book is to provide the reader with a simple, workable and memorable process that over time raises their performance on the job as well as their company to the next level—a higher peak. This gradual transformation occurs through improved thinking and behavioral modification resulting from knowledge, conviction and practice.

We all are who we are by nature, nurture and choice. This book will enhance (nurture) your gifts (nature) so that you can make better decisions (choice). You can then leverage these greater talents, increase your effectiveness and efficiency, be more satisfied, make more money, and help others more. You will, for example, realize that by sharpening your learning and promotional skills, you can create more and better innovations that more people will respond to and understand.

This book is intended to build upon the success you have already achieved. It has been written by a businessman for his fellow businessmen and women.

Chapter One

Reading Your Map

Everybody has their own unique career map and various routes they take in getting to their particular destination. Each one of us has a personality type, a thinking style and a predominate approach to life that guides our personal and professional lives.

As we strive to achieve peak performance in our businesses, it is critical to know our own maps and understand what motivates and directs our behavior every day on the job. We need to take a closer look at what is underneath the surface and behind the mask. In other words, why do we do what we do and how we go about doing it?

One simple system for gaining insight into what is behind our decision-making and actions is to analyze the five major approaches we use in seeking to bring about the best results for our companies. We call them the five *performance avenues* since they deal with the paths we take to succeed in all our endeavors.

These avenues include being a leader, a learner, an innovator, a manager, and a promoter. We all travel down each of these avenues, but spend more time on one or more than on the others. For example, you may be a great learner, but not a very good innovator, or be a super promoter, but a poor manager. We may spend a lot of time leading, but could lead more effectively if we had more knowledge and practiced the art of innovation to a greater extent.

The first step after opening your map is to determine your current location. This process amounts to an evaluation of your strengths and weaknesses as they relate to the five performance avenues. As you read through the next five chapters, envision yourself as a leader, a learner, an innovator, a manager, and a promoter and assess how much time and energy you spend on each avenue in running your business. Review the performance types in Chapter Seven and be prepared to take the Despard Performance Type Test in Chapter Eight to gain the self-knowledge of how you perform at work.

Types and Styles

Knowing your personality type is a critical success factor for both you and your business because it allows you to understand how you interact with people and how you think, act and view the world. There are no right or wrong types, but each one has its strengths and weaknesses. Your success in business depends in part on how well your career matches your personality type.

The most commonly used psychological test to determine your personality is the Myers-Briggs Type Indicator (MBTI). Jean Kummerow, Nancy Barger and Linda Kirby in *Work Types* relate that this system places everyone into one of 16 personality types based on four sets of preferences: (a) getting and using their energy by being an introvert or an extrovert, (b) gathering and taking in information with their senses or intuition, (c) making decisions by thinking or by feeling, and (d) organizing their lives by structure or spontaneity and flexibility. There are many excellent articles and books written on this subject.

Robert Benafri in *Understanding and Changing Your Management Style* confirms the importance of knowing your personality, or "psychological type" as he calls it, and points out that there are six elements that make up one's management style including: "psychological type (how we perceive and judge the world around us), need patterns (what drives us and how we gain a sense of personal satisfaction and competence), power bases (how we influence others), style of handling conflict and solving problems, personal values and their effect on organizational behavior and methods of handling stress." He emphasizes the need to identify and integrate all of these elements in evaluating yourself and to, as needed, rearrange them to create a different management style.

It is also important to know which side of your brain is dominant so that you understand where you channel most of your energies and in what area you need assistance from others with an opposite brain dominance. One well-known method is the Herrmann Brain Dominance Instrument (HBDI) that was created and developed by Ned Herrmann while he was a manager at General Electric. This survey identifies and measures the preferences and distinctions in one's major thinking styles attributed to the two sides of the brain. The dominant characteristics of the left brain are logic, analysis, technology, problem solving, planning, and organizing. Those of the right brain are imagination, creativity, artistic expression, emotion, conceptualizing, and communication.

Knowing what underlies our personality type, management and thinking styles can help reveal to us in which of the five performance avenues—leader, learner, innovator, manager, or promoter—we are most comfortable and are likely to be most effective. It will also tell us where we need the most help to fill in the gaps that hold us back from reaching the ultimate goal of peak performance on the job.

Emotional Intelligence

We all have an IQ, but we also have an emotional competence often referred to as our emotional intelligence that has been well researched by in Daniel Goleman, author of *Working with Emotional Intelligence*. Emotional intelligence (EQ) begins with an awareness of the scope and intensity of the key emotions and feelings that underlie our thinking and motivate our behavior.

Secondly, it is the degree of self-control we experience over these emotions and the adaptability we have in using them effectively. For example, is your anger personal and unrestrained or purposeful and controlled?

And lastly, emotional intelligence is our ability in handling relationships by being aware of others' feelings, needs and concerns and our skill in inducing desirable responses from others. Your emotional intelligence can be assessed, developed and applied to the crucial people-to- people exchanges of everyday business activity.

Evaluating Yourself

What makes you tick? You already have a good idea of who you are and what motivates you. A little more analysis using the checklist below will help you read your own map better and put your personal and professional life in perspective.

- What is your family, emotional, spiritual, social and educational background?
- What are your most significant strengths and weaknesses?

4

- Is your life in balance? Is workaholism a problem for you?
- Have time management and stress become personal challenges for you?
- How willing are you to make some changes in your life, if necessary?
- How do you make decisions and give important things priority?
- Can you afford your current lifestyle? Are you a spender or saver?
- Does a moral compass that includes character and integrity guide your life?
- Are you using your gifts and talents to the fullest extent possible?
- Are you willing to evaluate a list of your personal needs, wants, interests and goals.
- How does your personal life affect your professional life and vice versa?

Something must be defined and measured before it can be improved. Your self-evaluation provides you with the knowledge baseline for making the changes that may be necessary in meeting future challenges in both your personal and professional life.

Your Dominant Avenues

Now you are ready to start defining and measuring which of the five avenues you use the most as you drive to Performance Peak. The next five chapters of this book will each provide you with a "Destination" section that describes each avenue and "Directions" sections on how to improve on each one. At the end of each chapter are two inspiring examples of historical figures whose dominant avenue discussed in that chapter was their primary path to exceptional performance.

As you travel along the five avenues, you will see how each one is distinct and how they relate to each other. You can confirm what you believe is your dominate avenue and see if is too dominant while others too weak. Your dominant avenue is your most comfortable mode of operation and the one you spend the most time and energy on. It is also the one you expect everybody else to be on—the manager is frustrated with people who don't manage and the innovator with those who don't innovate.

Also look for your second most dominant or "secondary" avenue. Your two most dominant avenues are combined to determine your performance type. In the final four chapters, we will explain performance types, provide a test to determine your own type, discuss balancing and blending all five avenues, and prescribe how to arrive at and stay on top of Performance Peak, the ultimate destination for you and your business enterprise.

Chapter Two

Leader Avenue

Destination

There are a ton of books about leadership. One of the best examples is Noel Tichy's *Transformational Leader* that summarizes six characteristics of leaders as being change agents, courageous, believers in people, values driven, life-long learners, and having the ability to deal with complexity, ambiguity and uncertainty. In this Destination section we have provided a simple boiled-down definition of what it is to be a leader categorized in three sections—vision, climate and conversion. Examine the capability you have in this area and how much effort you put forth on this avenue to success.

Vision

A leader creates and communicates a purpose, a vision, a strategy and a plan. Leaders are always asking the question, "Where are we going?" and are enthusiastic pathfinders. Michael Dell in *Direct from Dell, Strategies that Revolu-*

tionized an Industry proclaims:

> I knew what I wanted to do: build better computers than IBM, offer great value and service to our customers by selling direct, and become number one in our industry.

It's the visionary that projects into the future and sees things others do not. They seek out new perspectives, use their imaginations, and dream of what could be. They have positive attitudes and see obstacles as worthy challenges to be met. They encourage, inspire and guide. In short, *they get followers. And in the process they discover and train other leaders.*

The leader's vision has to stretch everyone in their individual tasks, but be attainable. It also has to be shared and agreed to by the whole team without hesitation. It creates excitement and sets a high level of anticipation. In working towards the company's vision, a sense that we are all on a mission is achieved. This mission must then be stated clearly as a way to communicate where we have been, where we are now and where we are going.

Leadership is also about authority, power, command, and control that at their best flow naturally and intuitively from the leader himself and not from his title or position. A true leader has earned the right to lead and create the vision.

Climate

After establishing the vision, leaders lead by creating the right climate for the company that results in the greatest effectiveness and fulfillment. This is often termed the work environment or corporate culture and provides the ways and means for everyone to succeed.

The following is a listing of and a brief commentary on

the seven key elements of what makes up the climate that maximizes the synergy and potential of any organization.

Subordination. This is number one right out of the box. It is crucial to the climate of leadership that the leader subordinate his or her personal needs and agendas for the greater good. In other words, the leader's needs and agendas may not be the most desirable ones for the business.

The leader has to satisfy some of their personal needs outside the workplace and modify their agendas to better suit the company and its strategy and goals. This often takes courage and maturity, but the followers will readily notice that the leader is more interested in the well being of the whole company rather than just their personal part of it.

Humility. The best leaders have a sincere sense of humility. They keep their egos in check and realize that they don't know it all. They create a climate of friendliness, equality and respect that provides a corporate comfort zone for more meaningful interaction.

They are subtly and patiently assertive, not openly aggressive. They can swallow their pride and laugh at themselves. Leaders know that the power of their own humility enables them to influence others more deeply and guide them more effectively.

Expectations and Examples. The setting forth of clear behavioral and performance expectations of the leader, the employees, business associates and the company results in a much less stressful work environment. It limits organizational confusion so the whole team can concentrate on the mission at hand. Effective leaders communicate their expectations consistently and by both formal and informal audio and visual approaches.

They also communicate the degree of corporate integrity

and character to the rest of the organization by their own example. Action speaks much louder than words in the example the leader sets in the area of values. The leader is the needle of a company's moral compass—where they go in terms of ethics, so goes the company.

Fact versus Fiction. The leader needs to establish the basic rules of the road regarding the facts of any given situation. Facts and figures don't lie and, in the end, they rule over the fiction of unreliable promises, possibilities and projections.

Once this principle is part of the corporate climate, except for an occasional firm reminder, it won't have to be addressed very much in the future. Everyone will be telling the truth, the whole truth, and nothing but the truth or telling their story to someone else in another company.

The Whole Brain. You have heard it many times, but think about it again. *Isn't the whole brain of a company smarter than each individual brain?* Aren't ten or a hundred heads better than one?

The term synergy refers to the concept that the sum of the parts is better than any one part. Creating a climate of synergy means leading the group to its highest peak performance by combining the efforts and input of all the stakeholders in an enterprise. And that yields addition and multiplication, not subtraction and division. It means waves of the same length traveling together and reinforcing one another.

Consensus Building. There is nearly always a consensus in any organization and it is up to the leader to find it, formulate it and communicate it to all concerned both inside and outside of the company. Where there is a corporate will, there is a corporate way. Leaders get everybody behind the consensus and have a rally at "the commons"—the common ground somewhere in the center of the town.

The lack of leadership subordination and humility mentioned above prevents the determination of a genuine consensus on innovations and circumstances as they arise. The leader needs to continually focus on gaining the majority opinion of a group within a climate of non-threatening interaction, though that may occur at times with a dose of healthy friction. Everyone's thoughts and ideas must be actively solicited and given a fair hearing.

The Changing Climate. The only thing that is constant is change. In fact, companies over time have only two options—lose or change. The leader needs to create a climate where change is a constructive opportunity rather than a threat and where new ideas are always welcome.

The leader is the facilitator and the catalyst. He or she encourages everybody to experiment and not be afraid of failing. A climate of change makes change the norm and reduces its chaos and frustration.

From these seven elements, we can see the importance of climate control and its effect on the atmosphere in the workplace. The leader has to keep checking the temperature of the organization and make sure it is success-friendly.

Conversion

After vision and climate, the third aspect of the definition of leadership is conversion. The new converts—the leader's ardent followers—are well motivated and eager to perform at their peak. If the leader has created the right vision and the right climate and says "Follow me!", the converts will gladly follow. Some of these converts will even become new leaders.

The leader and the followers form a team that becomes

proficient at turning the best ideas into reality. Together they become high achievers and can stretch their abilities to meet new challenges. They understand the positive implications of the win/win philosophy both inside and outside of the organization. To convert is to persuade someone to adopt a particular belief and transform them in the process. True converts stay the course and are a tremendous asset to any business. Their leader has given them reason to believe in him or her and in the company's vision and mission. These converts in turn help to convert other new recruits that come into the organization thereby making conversion an ongoing process.

In concluding this Destination section, we have seen what the essence of leadership is in terms of vision, climate, and conversion. In the next section on "Directions," we will take a look at how leaders actually lead their people on a day-to-day basis.

Directions

Leaders manifest their leadership in four specific areas: *futuring, socializing, coaching,* and *benefiting.* These are the key ways leaders create a vision and strategy for their organization and the skills they need to develop in order to motivate and energize their followers.

Futuring

As we discussed in the earlier section on vision, leaders must think through how to best take their company into the future. It can be for one, three, five, ten years, or more. The tools for futuring include *strategic thinking, seeking new challenges,* and *realistic forecasting.*

Strategic Thinking. As I point out in my guidebook, *The Strategic Thinking Process for Home Builders*, the purpose of a strategy is to be *effective by doing the right things* whereas the purpose of a business plan is to be *efficient by doing things right*. It is the leader's responsibility to see that their company is doing the right things now and in the future. Strategizing is a vital and dynamic process that is in constant motion.

Every business is different and requires its own tailor-made strategy. Answering the following questions will help you create the strategy that is most appropriate for your company:

- What makes your company successful?
- What strategies have worked well for you in the past? For your competition?
- What makes a particular strategy successful?
- What should your company be the best at doing?
- How will your strategy make your company different?
- How long do your strategies typically last?
- How quickly can you change your strategy if it is not working?
- Are you more comfortable with a low risk/ reward strategy or one that emphasizes high risks and high rewards?
- Are you looking for new opportunities that may require new strategies?
- How will you measure the results of your strategy?

Work with a group of your key associates to develop a complete response to each question. Then proceed to the next phase—formulating your business strategy. Here is a list of steps you can take to do that:

- Define exactly who your customers really are.
- Explain why they buy your products and services.
- List the parts of your business that promise to have the highest profit margin.
- Consider ways to emphasize and promote your core competency — that is, what you do best.
- Determine the ways you make money the fastest and with the least amount of effort and financial risk.
- State your existing sustainable competitive advantages and identify ways to create new ones.
- Figure out several ways in which your company does not have to compete head-on with your competitors.
- Devise the methods and means by which your people and financial resources can be put to the highest and best use.
- Make a prioritized breakdown of the most effective strategy for your company over the next three years.
- Test your strategy with those who have a stake in the success of your business.
- Finalize your strategy and communicate it to your staff and business associates.
- Check your strategy in six months to see if it is still the best one for your company. Modify it as necessary.

One of the most important strategic concepts in business is to be different from your competition. Robert Goizueta, former CEO of Coca-Cola, once declared, "In real estate, it's location, location, location. In business it's differentiate,

differentiate, differentiate." Jack Trout in The *Power of Simplicity* states that differentiating yourself comes in three parts:

1. Having a simple idea that separates you from your competition.

2. Having the credentials or the product that makes this concept real and believable.

3. Building a program to make your customers and prospects aware of this difference.

Trout further offers excellent advice about the alternative to being different when he asserts, "In a world where everyone is after your business you must *supply your customers with a reason to buy from you instead of from your competitor.* If you don't offer that reason, then you had better offer a very good price." *In other words, be different or be cheap.*

Seeking New Challenges. Leaders must be out ahead and scouting for new challenges—both conventional and nonconventional opportunities that stretch their organization. They have to know and communicate to their followers that the unprecedented and seemingly impossible may be the next and most rewarding challenge. They must further instill the confidence that their company can do things their competitors cannot do.

Realistic Forecasting. Realistic forecasting simply means that a leader must be analytical and objective in their assessment of what their business can achieve in the short and long term. They have to be sure that a realistic business plan can be prepared and implemented from the proposed strategy, opportunities, and challenges.

This assessment involves current and future financial capability, credible development of your people and an honest prediction of relevant economic and competitive market forces. *A strategy cannot be envisioned in a vacuum.* A realistic forecast is a summary of the right things to be doing backed up by a way to get them done.

Socializing

Social skills are a major part of our emotional intelligence quotient and are more important than most leaders are willing to admit and take time to develop. *The leader has to be a limited friend, that is, a friend with well-defined limits that allow for respect and discipline.* Leaders have to be likeable and learn how to get along with those they do not naturally like.

It simply starts with an attitude that says you want your partners, associates and employees to like you—to be at ease around you, to share things with you, attend company social events with you, exchange interests with you, laugh with you, and so on. There is no specific formula, but keeping the likeability factor in mind at all times will do it. You pretty well know whether or not they like you.

Likeability is a two-way street. If you don't like someone, fake it for now, but learn to like them. They will sense any negative thoughts or feelings you have about them. Look at their good points, talk to them as friends, find common ground, and concentrate on what you do like about them.

And finally the art of successful socializing includes a leader's genuine attitude of understanding and caring about others and their feelings and interests. Developing a sense of empathy and appropriately demonstrating it to your associates, particularly in the tough personal and professional times, is the sign of a mature leader.

Coaching

The most noticeable daily operational activity of leaders is coaching. Nothing is more important in getting the job done than being a great coach. The following is a breakdown of the vital components of how to be a winning coach.

Listening. *Active listening, that is. Before a coach can begin to coach at all, he or she has to absorb the knowledge of those they are coaching—by not just hearing them, but listening to them.* It's a matter of focused attention on the information coming in without the distraction of thinking of something else or getting ready to say something yourself.

A good listener asks the right questions. This reveals the underlying causes of what is being communicated by a person's speech, body language and facial expressions. Real listening is about understanding and processing what is heard, responding to it and storing it for future use.

Teaching. You have probably heard it said that, "Give a man a fish and you feed him for a day; teach him to fish and you feed him for a lifetime." Teaching is about imparting knowledge and demonstrating skills to someone else so that they can perform as well or even better than you can. The next step, training, is teaching that becomes learned behavior through a disciplined program.

Great coaches are great teachers and trainers because they realize it makes winners. The best coaches also teach well because they care about and want to help improve those they are coaching. Teaching can be an important source of energy and enthusiasm for a coach who is especially gratified by good results.

Criticizing. Catch someone doing something really well, praise and encourage him quickly and emphatically. Catch someone doing something poorly or wrong, point it out to them in a respectful but firm manner with the expectation of learning from it and improving their performance.

The way a leader evaluates the troops to their faces is more important than most leaders realize. How the troops perceive what the leader thinks of them can drastically affect their job performance. So the way in which both positive and negative criticism is administered is absolutely critical.

Great coaches are cheerleaders and reinforcers who dwell far more on the good things than the bad things. There is a strong need in our human nature for being told we are doing a good job. One's response is equally strong and provides a huge source of essentially free energy.

But people do not inherently want "yes" coaches who only praise, credit and validate. They expect to be accountable for their actions and want effective and honest criticism as they strive to improve their work. But be specific and avoid the blame game.

Team Building. OK, you have heard about this concept until you are blue in the face! But check out these simple team attributes to test and see if you are a team builder or a team builder wannabe.

- My team is better than any member of the team.
- It's safe to try and fail on our team.
- All the members are running in the same direction.
- All members abide by the same rules.
- Credit for a member's idea is important, but not nearly as important as the idea.
- Decisions are made with some kind of input from all of the members.
- Once agreed upon, all members get behind a

decision.
- Members understand, respect and get along with each other.
- Members excite and challenge each other.
- The team is equal to the sum of its members.
- The team wants to win.
- The results are the team's results.

Great coaches build great teams even without great team members. They have a way of putting the interests of the team first and the team member second, of getting the best out of each member, and giving the credit to the whole team. Coach "K", Mike Krzyzewski, Duke University's famed basketball coach put it this way:

> If you develop your business as a team where everybody in the business feels like it is theirs, you create ownership. If something is yours, you treat it better, protect it, work at it, and love it.

Mediating. This is the least favorite role of a coach, but there are situations where mediation has to be done and done well. And it must take place before a dispute, festering as it always will, gets worse. It starts with honest and complete communication and a definition of the differences.

Mediation basically involves objectively evaluating the thoughts, feelings, interests, positions, and goals of both sides. Alternatives and options are then put forth until both sides agree and are ready, willing and able to keep the agreement. The coach has to decisively intercede at the right time and in the right way. *The goal must always be a win/win outcome.*

Passion. Not just any kind of passion, but passion that is enthusiastic and contagious and that inspires and energizes others to their absolute attainable peak performance. Don't go into coaching or any kind of leadership if you don't have a deep commitment from the heart to create a vision and carry out a mission. Your team is always taking your temperature and if it is ever lukewarm, they will know it right away. If it is red hot, they will know that too!

Passionate coaches are always "going for it" and doing the impossible. They don't take no for an answer and don't like failure. They care a lot about each team member and about what can be achieved. *Coaches are dreamers, drill sergeants, doctors and drummers all in one.*

Benefiting

At the end of the day a leader has to look out for everyone's well being—the total benefits of working for a particular company. *A less than holistic approach to leadership is shortsighted and may be short-lived.* This concept can be centered around two major themes. The first is the spirit of an organization that affects the heart, mind and even at times the body of each individual. The second is compensation, the universal motivator and measure of success that has the practical power to drive people and businesses.

Spirit. The psychology of the work environment is as complex as the mind itself. *How an employee or associate perceives how they are being treated by the leader is of paramount importance.* Thoughts and feelings matter, and matter a lot. Attitude, they say, is everything—and performance is directly tied to it.

Organizational morale is within each individual before it becomes a group attitude. Leaders need to know what their people think and feel. *A good mental attitude is an essential benefit, one that is not costly to provide, but one that is very costly not to provide.* There are many ways of improving morale including emphasizing the positive, sharing exciting victories, injecting lots of appropriate humor, exercising patience and being consistently values-based.

William Thompson, president of The Spirited Workplace, a consulting firm that specializes in developing the spiritual side of businesses has found that:

> The reality is that a company where employees have a genuine sense of calling and balance in their lives, they are respected by management, they are encouraged to act ethically and honestly, the company compensates them well because they are persons of value, where the diversity of various ethnic groups is honored...is a good place to work.

The esprit de corps of your company is established by the committed visioning, climate creation, futuring, socializing and coaching from the heart that we have covered in this chapter. Great leadership is about instilling a healthy and happy corporate spirit and mindset—one person at a time.

Compensation. And now for the financial part. *Compensation is extremely important and leaders must use it effectively to have totally willing employees.* Here is a basic list of ways to benefit your people through their compensation package:

- Emphasize the bonus/incentive compensation rather than the salary.
- The bonus must reflect two things—how well the company has performed in the past period and how well the employee/associate has done.
- Tie the bonus to pre-set targeted goals.
- Surprise raises and bonuses are the most appre-

ciated.
- The effect of raises and bonuses does not last as long as you think.
- Check out compensation packages in your industry and other industries.
- Show each individual a list of all their financial benefits including an annual grand total.
- Remember you can always raise but rarely lower the compensation package.
- Help your people keep more of what they earn by tax avoidance programs and benefits.
- Help them save for the future with a great profit sharing plan (do not call it a retirement plan).
- Increase non-financial benefits that do not cost you a lot.

On the one hand money is a commodity, but on the other, it is a powerful motivator that leaders must use carefully and consistently. *Compensation speaks volumes about how your people provide for themselves and their families, how they are validated as good workers and how they are appreciated for what they do.*

Leaders need to know a lot about the best use of money in motivating their employees and associates. One way to do that is to simply ask their people once in a while how money motivates them to do better and how they prefer to be compensated. Another way is to observe their reactions to changes in any of their financial benefits. And keep in mind at all times what Jon Katzenbach relates in *Peak Performance, Aligning the Hearts and Minds of Your Employees*, "Employees' entrepreneurial spirit is energized when their rewards are linked tightly to their output."

A leader's followers will, as they say, "follow the money" wherever it goes. There are many other important benefits available to your employee/associates, but remember, cash is still king for most of them in the long run. However, if and when it turns to greed, it's time to re-evaluate and reflect on nobler virtues.

Therefore, doing what leaders do involves optimistically but realistically looking into the near and distant future. It also involves developing your social habits and being a great coach. Whether or not leading is your dominant avenue, sharpening your leadership skills will improve your performance on the four other avenues.

Lincoln's Legendary Leadership

Abraham Lincoln was indeed an extraordinary leader whose unwavering prudence, fortitude and hope won the war that kept our nation together. Newspaperman Horace Greeley once wrote the following description of Lincoln:

> He was not a born king of men.....but a child of the common people, who made himself a great persuader, therefore a leader, by dint of **firm resolve**, **patient effort**, and **dogged perseverance**. He slowly won his way to eminence and fame by **doing the work that lay next to him**—doing it **with all his growing might**—doing it **as well as he could**, and **learning by his failures**, when failures were encountered, how to do it better.....He was **open to all impressions and influences**, and gladly profited by the teaching of events and circumstances, no matter how adverse or unwelcome. There was probably no year in his life when he was not a **wiser, cooler, and better** man then he had been the year preceding.

Coach Lombardi and the Power of Passion

Vince Lombardi is believed by many to be the greatest

football coach of all time. He won 74% of his games in his professional football coaching career. Of all the many leadership qualities he had, it was the power of his passion that lead his Green Bay Packers to be one of the best teams in professional football history. Passion has a way of intensifying a leader's other gifts and talents and enhances their ability to highly motivate their followers to stretch and strive for peak performance.

His passion was contagious. There was passionate teaching, training and equipping that resulted in passionate learning, conditioning, and preparedness that resulted in superior strategies, precise execution, and sustained performance. And that resulted in a culture of victory and attaining the goal of the team—winning football games in an ethical and sportsmanlike manner. As Lombardi himself was known for saying, "Winning is not everything, it is the only thing." And he said it with passion.

Chapter Three

Learner Avenue

Destination

As mentioned in the last chapter, learning makes us better leaders. It also makes us better innovators, managers and promoters. Successful business people spend a lot of time on Learner Avenue where the dividend payoff is very high. The more you know, the more you will achieve. This is true in any personal or professional endeavor. Michael Dell in *Direct From Dell, Strategies that Revolutionized an Industry* asserts:

> Look at learning as a necessity, not a luxury. With business moving at such a fast pace, it doesn't take much to get behind in today's market place. Today's leaders are voracious learners.

In the Destination section of this chapter, we have provided a definition of learning by creating the three-phase *Learning Ladder*—an overview of the progression from raw data to that which actually transforms us, and those we seek to transform.

We will then answer the question, "Why learn?"

The Learning Ladder

In Phase I of the *Learning Ladder* we acquire *data, history, information,* and *knowledge.* In Phase II, we process Phase I and add value with *understanding, practical intelligence, wisdom,* and *conviction.* And finally in Phase III, we use Phase II to *influence, change,* and *transform.*

Phase I. *Data* is raw facts and figures. *History* is the events of the past. *Information* is organized and analyzed data and history. *Knowledge* adds observation, research, education, reasoning and experience to information.

There is so much data, history, information, and knowledge available that we must devise ways to be selective and focus on learning channels that direct us to what we really need and want. Prioritizing is critical to managing the constant flow of Phase I learning, particularly in establishing the data bank that initiates the whole learning process.

Knowledge is a web that is interrelated, integrated and interdependent. We can, therefore, induce and apply significant specific knowledge from a broad general knowledge of the world and how it works. For example, if you have a sophisticated knowledge of national and international economics, you are in a better position to be a successful investor in our complex modern stock markets. Knowledge of all kinds moves us from taking chances to taking calculated risks.

Determine what data, history, information and knowledge you must learn to be effective, go and learn it and keep on learning it. *Know more than your competition and you will win.*

Phase II. *Understanding* is adding reflection, meaning and emotional awareness to knowledge, and realizing its implications and potential. *Practical intelligence* is common sense knowledge and understanding that you are ready to apply to your decisions and behavior. *Wisdom* is perspective, discernment, choices, and moral judgment. *Conviction* is being truly convinced of and committed to what you believe.

T. S. Eliot wrote, "We know too much and are convinced of too little." Too much of the time we get from knowledge to conviction the hard way—with great pain, suffering and loss. It is a challenge to acquire a lot of knowledge, but a greater challenge to process it with understanding and practical application. And what about exercising wisdom—the top of the knowledge chain?

Proverbs 3:13 says, "Blessed is he who finds wisdom, the man who gains understanding, for she is more profitable than silver and yields better returns than gold." We need to spend enough time on Learner Avenue checking our moral compass to have the wisdom to use sound judgment and make the best choices.

When we get to the next step, conviction, we have arrived at a point that drives—or at least should drive—our decision making process. That's why what we are convicted or convinced of is so important—what we think, say, and do is a result of our convictions. And deeper and more firmly grounded convictions provide for a straighter and clearer direction.

Phase III. *Influencing* is communicating your convictions and winning people over. *Change* is new and different circumstances, attitudes and management systems. *Transformation* of people and companies occurs when significant changes—paradigm shifts—are tested and refined and when newly formed habits are put into action.

Phase III is the most difficult to accomplish and is where most failures occur. You know what to do, but not exactly how to get it done. The manager and promoter in you must now take over and the chapters on Manager Avenue and Promoter Avenue directly address this challenge.

In thinking about learning itself, realize that there is indeed a ladder from the simple to the complex and that value is added in each of the three phases described above. *Once we get our facts straight and have enough information, we can become knowledgeable, understanding, and then wise. This is followed by positive change that becomes permanent through transformation that forms new habits.*

Why Learn?

Learning will often make or break a business. Learning is needed to keep ahead of the competition, to make smart choices and reduce mistakes. The learning process—from data to transformation—must be a continuous ongoing process. It can only stop if you know it all.

Did you ever see a competitor do something that you should be doing? How did they get ahead? Did they know something you did not know? That is why learning as much as you can about your industry and your markets is so important.

As we can readily see, learning affects our decision-making. The goal according to John Hammond, Ralph Keeney and Howard Raiffa in *Smart Choices*, is to make smart choices by seeking more alternatives that are the raw materials of decision-making. They point out that a decision is no better than the best alternative that is considered. We don't usually get the best answer when we only look at a few alternatives.

And lastly, mistakes in business are often costly—very costly. They may even drag your company down and prevent you from taking advantage of a great opportunity because you are dealing with a serious problem. The more we know, the less the risk of making mistakes.

Directions

We learn through our five senses and in many different ways, and in varying amounts. We learn a lot through unconscious absorption and imitation. Learning never stops and is a significant source of energy for most people, particularly for those who love to learn.

In business as in the rest of life, learning comes before growth and improvement. The strategy is to create a learning environment that focuses primarily on the fundamentals and fosters becoming knowledge specialists in our field of endeavor. In doing so, we need to create, acquire and transfer knowledge that best promises to modify our behavior and that of those in our sphere of influence.

How we learn in the business world can be broken down into eight major categories that include researching, understanding people, benchmarking, learning from your customers, competition, and mistakes, utilizing wisdom, and finally, conviction. These are steps in a learning system and it takes consistent discipline to produce meaningful results.

Researching. Research learning includes basic education and training as well as exploring unknown areas and sailing into uncharted waters. It is also about experimenting by "pushing the envelope" and creating new knowledge for your company to use.

Casual research will not tell you much more than what a lot of people know, but serious research puts you ahead of the pack. Think of it as searching and then re-searching— that is, searching again only deeper. Read aggressively, study in short bursts, be more observant, and exercise your memory. You know how to go about this, but may not have spent enough time on it.

Understanding People. In Chapter One, Reading Your Map, we emphasized the importance of evaluating yourself. It is also critical to your success to devise a methodology to evaluate as well as understand your employees and business associates. What makes them tick, what are their hot buttons, and what is their psychological profile and level of emotional intelligence?

You need to have a working knowledge of their personality type, management and thinking styles, interests and goals. Observe them, read their body language and faces, determine what motivates them, and understand how they make decisions. What is the most effective way for you to interact with them?

Benchmarking. This is simply discovering what the best practices are in your industry on a national basis and putting them into practice in your own company. Benchmarking is a constant learning experience that comes about through active observation of your industry.

Such things as publications, trade shows, seminars, networking, and getting out in the field are some ways of determining the best practices. There may also be those best practices in another industry that you can apply to yours. For example, a homebuilder can check out the benchmarking of the automobile industry and get proven practices such as effective sales programs that can help them in their homebuilding business.

Learning From Your Customers. Are you proactively listening to your customers? If you are listening, are you learning from them? But this type of learning is also about knowing what your customers want even before they do.

Great learners figure out what their customers are thinking and what causes them to buy their products through formal and informal surveys of all kinds. They do whatever is required to take their customer's pulse. All you have to do is ask and they will tell you. Market research charts the course for product development—without it, you don't really know where to go next.

Learning From Your Competition. This is obvious, but we often don't do enough investigating on what our competition is up to. Do such things as pretending you are one of their customers, studying their ads and literature, or writing down what you think are the highlights of their three-year business plan.

Your competition may be doing something you should be doing. You need to know what they are doing to be sure to differentiate your operations and products from theirs. And you want to be the best, but who and what are you to be better than?

Learning From Your Mistakes. Tom Watson Jr. of IBM said, "If you want to succeed, double your failure rate." It's hard to argue with the concept that experience is the best teacher. And it is our mistakes and failures that teach us the most—as long as we are not defensive and self-righteous—because of the pain, suffering and loss we often go through when something goes wrong.

But since similar circumstances surrounding a mistake may come up again, we must analyze the root causes of each mistake and permanently change our behavior and systems to prevent its reoccurrence. A big mistake is not making any, but a bigger mistake is not learning from them. *History does not have to repeat itself! And we must also be able to forgive ourselves, put mistakes in the back of our minds and go forward as a more experienced and knowledgeable person.*

Utilizing Wisdom. This is a tough one that takes some real soul searching. Wisdom is ultimately derived from a

transcendent morality such as biblical codes and standards of conduct. "CW" means conventional wisdom, but also think of it as "classical wisdom" that has successfully stood the test of three millennia of human experience.
William J. Bennett in *The Moral Compass* puts it this way:

> Philosophers, theologians, and poets have long regarded wisdom as the sibling virtue of morality. If an individual is to do good, the tenets of the heart must be informed and directed by a well ordered mind. In fact, the classical Greek thinkers regarded prudence as one of the fundamental virtues; to them, the word meant not circumspection, as it does today, but rather the ability to govern and discipline oneself by the use of reason. It meant being able to recognize the right choice in specific circumstances, and it was the intellectual virtue that made it possible to put the moral virtues into action.

Why reinvent the wheel? Study those who have been wise in the past. What did they do right? Make judgments carefully and consider all the consequences of your choices and decisions. How does what you will do affect others? Patiently think things through and seek the advice and counsel of others. *Wisdom adds untold value to our personal and professional lives.*

Conviction. We are convicted—that is truly convinced—when the learning process finally affects our thinking and changes our behavior. Why did T. S. Eliot say we are convinced of too little? Is it that we must have things pounded into our brains somehow?

Being convicted of something takes a thorough analysis of Phases I and II of the *Learning Ladder*, experimental application through trial and error and a consistent commitment to what we believe to be the truest and best. A person of conviction is one who has diligently sought the right path and who lives and works with a set of principles that are based on life's lessons and "classical wisdom."

In concluding the Directions section of this chapter, learn as much as you can (we use only about 10% of our brains), as fast and easily as you can, and derive satisfaction from doing it. Continually challenge yourself by going up the *Learning Ladder* one rung at a time and add value with each rung. We can then apply—and we have to learn how best to do that—what we have learned in effectively and efficiently building better businesses.

The Preparation of Captain Lewis

Learning is about being prepared, and nobody could possibly have been better prepared than Meriwether Lewis who, along with William Clark, traversed what would one day be the entire United States of America with the Lewis and Clark Expedition. As insightfully chronicled by Stephen E. Ambrose in his epic *Undaunted Courage*, it was President Thomas Jefferson, a learner of learners, who in 1803 insisted that Lewis know everything then known that might be useful in achieving such an awesome goal.

Lewis, for example, went to Harpers Ferry to learn about and obtain the latest in weaponry; to Lancaster, PA to learn about surveying; and to Philadelphia to learn about dry goods, timekeeping and medicine. He had to study botany, zoology, astronomy, map-making, boat-building, diary-keeping, native American cultures and much more. The expedition needed all this practical and invaluable knowledge along with Captain Clark's wisdom and military experience to survive the unexpected dangers of the harsh, lonely, and endless wilderness.

Jefferson knew that the expedition would not be successful without this kind of preparation. He was right. In business as in the rest of life, we cannot learn too much or be too well prepared.

Learning From Failure—Edsel to Mustang

With big cars in fashion in 1952 Henry Ford II decided that Ford Motor Company needed a full-size car with a more daring design. He created a new car division to make a new model car that came to be called the Edsel after his uncle Edsel Ford, Henry Ford's brother who died in 1943. The company had great hopes for the new 1958 Edsels that were delivered to showrooms in the fall of 1957. The many innovations in engineering, luxury, and styling and a massive ad campaign promised to make the Edsel a big success for Ford. But it never caught on. Sales for the first year were projected to be 200,000, but only 110,847 Edsels were made before production ended in 1960. A recession, manufacturing problems, a general distaste for the car's styling and lifestyle changes doomed the Edsel to failure.

Learning a lot from this infamous mistake, Ford conducted much more thorough and insightful marketing research over the next several years before creating other new models including the Thunderbird and the Mustang. The sporty Mustang dubbed the "working man's Thunderbird" was introduced in 1964 and was available as a hardtop or a convertible. This classic car swept the country with world record sales of 418,000 in its first year with nearly three million sold by 1973. The year 2000 marks its 36th anniversary of production with styling that has remained similar to its original design including a galloping chrome pony on the grille.

The importance of learning before doing something and in particular, learning from your prior mistakes is glaringly clear with these two Ford models—one a huge mistake, one a huge success. In the Edsel case too many assumptions were made with too little research of the general appeal of Edsel's radically new design. In the case of the Mustang, Ford tapped a whole new, growing, and enthusiastic segment of the car market. The company keeps learning from its customers and keeps selling Mustangs.

Chapter Four

Innovator Avenue

Destination

There is an innovative side to all of us, but some kind of prompting is often necessary to go to higher and higher levels. *Innovation is practical applied creativity.* It's creative thought that has been processed to the point where it can be successfully put to use in your business.

Creativity actually starts on Learner Avenue since to be creative, we must always be on the road to discovery and sensitive to all that is around us. We then fit the pieces of the puzzle together in a new and different way.

Creativity is an original energetic force that flows by design from the existing to the newly formed. It involves unrealized and unprecedented thinking. It's the seed that precedes innovation, which then becomes the seedling that is fed and watered.

Innovation is a constant process that by definition always improves upon what already exists. It is not a mindless mutation or simply something that is different. It is revolutionary in nature, the engine of real progress, and well worth striving to achieve. Innovation can add unforeseen and incalculable value to people and companies.

So let's take a look at what innovation is and isn't. What do real innovators do anyway? We can start by defining the *art of innovation* in five parts—*dream machine, creating paradigms, bright ideas, engaging the chaos,* and *entrepreneurship.*

The Art of Innovation

Dream Machine. Being a dream machine is imagining what could be and indulging in possibility thinking that asks the questions, "What if this or what if that?" It recycles our past experiences and reassembles them to create new ones. It's letting the mind wonder, never being satisfied with the status quo and relentlessly seeking better ways of doing things. Albert Einstein once claimed that, "imagination is more important than knowledge."

Dreaming harnesses the vast power of your imagination to think out-of-the-box and come up with new and different approaches. Where there is a will there is a way and where there is a dream, there is an innovation. *Innovators are dreamers who turn dreams into inventions. If necessity is the mother of invention, imagination is the father.*

Creating a Paradigm. Creating a paradigm is creating new concepts and strategies that bring about major innovations that result in a paradigm shift in your business enterprise. These shifts, which need to occur every three to five years, involve global *big picture* type thinking that keeps a company on the cutting edge of an industry by making the right moves before everybody else does.

Creating a paradigm actually starts on Leader Avenue with the vision of what a business wants to become. It often takes new and different strategies and innovative paradigm shifts to get there.

Bright Ideas. You may believe that bright ideas just pop into peoples' heads, but actually in most cases, they have prepared their brains to come up with them. The innovator is constantly—both consciously and subconsciously—thinking about how to do things better by bright ideas, some of which actually become revolutionary breakthroughs.

Bright ideas are not an accident but the result of an innovative mindset and corporate culture. An exciting dynamic prevails when everybody is at least partially focused on the next bright idea, whoever may have it. The suggestion box is full, and before long your company is no longer "the business as we knew it." Computer innovator Michael Dell puts it this way:

> Our culture despises the status quo. We try to precondition our people to look for the breakthrough ideas, so that when we're confronted with big strategic challenges, they rise to the occasion and come up with the best solutions—fast.

Engaging the Chaos. A measure of chaos and confusion is inherent in all real and meaningful innovation. *Chaos results from the **unexpected**—not knowing the outcome beforehand, **experimentation**—trial and error/success and failure and **volatility**—financial as well as emotional highs and lows.*

Chaos through innovation usually causes restlessness, frustration and stress, but standing still can be as bad or worse. We must engage the chaos head-on in both our personal and professional lives, work with it, and actually use this kind of nervous energy and enthusiasm to our advantage.

Entrepreneurship. *Entrepreneurs are innovators because* *they are ready, willing and able to grow and change, search for opportunities, seek new ventures, take risks and see possibilities that others do not.* They make change their ally in doing battle against the competition.

They also continually reallocate resources to the highest and most profitable use, which is often a company's latest innovation. Money and other resources thereby support and spur innovation and keep it moving in the right direction.

Entrepreneurs are realistically creative and know how to make money through innovation—in fact, that is their business. The entrepreneur gets to the top of the food chain by eating and digesting all of the bright ideas down the line. It's ideas that put venture capital to work. As Roy Disney once said, "More money is not what we need around here because we can usually get it. What we need are more good ideas."

The Results of Innovation

When you continue to do what you have always done, you will get what you have always gotten. So without innovation, businesses will not meet their full potential and eventually lag behind their competitors. *Businesses have two choices—change or lose.*

Here's a list of the many positive benefits of creativity followed by innovation in your business:

- You will make more money by having new and more profitable profit centers.
- You will be able to charge more for your innovative products and services, especially when they are first introduced.
- You will stay ahead of your competition.
- You will be better able to sustain your business for the long term.
- Your company will be more comfortable with

growth and change both inside and outside of your company.
- One innovation often leads to another one.
- You and your associates will be more excited and energized about your business.
- Your people will experiment more, take more risks and not be afraid to fail.
- Your people will make more money and be more likely to stay with your company.
- Your customers will catch the excitement and buy more of your products and services.

Right? Now compare this list to one for a business that does not innovate on a regular basis! The difference is one between success and failure. Creativity and innovation are not optional. And they are not a terms that accountants use on your balance sheet, but it has a huge effect on your bottom line.

Directions

It is very hard to define and quantify innovation, but even harder to come up with a recipe of how best to go about it. It depends on you, your company and your type of industry. For example, you may have to conquer your own personality type that does not like change, a corporate culture that likes the status quo, or your company that is operating in an old-economy industry.

It is one thing to be an observer of other innovators, but a real challenge to be one yourself. Here are some general how-to concepts that promise to keep creativity flowing in your company and keep innovation where it belongs—on the front burner.

Attitude. You may have to overcome a certain level of

pessimism. In 1835 Lord Kelvin, President of the Royal Society, said that, "Heavier than air flying machines are impossible." In 1923 Robert Milikan, a Nobel prize winner in physics asserted, "There is no likelihood that man can ever tap the power of the atom."

And so a positive "Can Do!" (from the US Navy Seabees) attitude is critical to the creative thinking process. *You could start off by stating, "We are the innovators in our market and in our industry." Say it, believe it and do it!* Stretch your organization to new heights, but be careful to be realistic because unattainable goals can be discouraging. And take encouragement from W. Edwards Deming who said that, "Every activity is a process and can be improved."

Thinking. In the heat of the battle of your working life, you actually have to schedule time to think creatively about new ideas and innovations for your company. At no additional charge (that is, *for free*) the subconscious part of your brain will do this too—and to a greater degree if you tell it to do so by your conscious thoughts. The more you think, the more you will innovate. Thomas Watson once said, "The trouble with every one of us is that we do not think enough. Thought has been the father of every advance since time began."

In *The Power of Innovative Thinking, Let New Ideas Lead You to Success*, Jim Wheeler concludes that innovative thinkers:

- Use different ways to get results.
- Appear unorganized.
- Value the process more than the actual goal.
- Prefer to continue the process rather than reach the goal.
- Be involved in more than one activity or task at a time.

- Prefer to learn through more than one source.

Understand that thinking is often random and unsettling but takes discipline, patience and perseverance. Give your ideas time to evolve and don't be discouraged and abandon them too soon.

In his book *How to Think Like Leonardo da Vinci, Seven Steps to Genius Every Day*, Michael Gelb offers these seven Da Vincian principles on thinking:

- *Curiosity*. An insatiably curious approach to life and an unrelenting quest for continuous learning.

- *Testing*. A commitment to test knowledge through experience, persistence and a willingness to learn from mistakes.

- *Observation*. The continual refinement of the senses, especially sight, as the means to enliven experience.

- *Uncertainty*. A willingness to embrace ambiguity, paradox and uncertainty.

- *Art and Science*. The development of the balance between science and art, logic and imagination. "Whole-brain" thinking.

- *Fitness and Poise*. The cultivation of grace, ambidexterity, fitness and poise.

- *Interconnectedness*. A recognition of the appreciation for the interconnectedness of all things and phenomena. Systems thinking.

Practice. Create a corporate culture that practices innovation and makes it a priority. For example, keep the word "innovation" on your meeting agenda and talk it up at every opportunity. Leave no doubt in anyone's mind that your company practices innovation everyday.

Outline an innovation system that everyone can follow that includes how new ideas are communicated, criticized, tested, and refined. *Provide a budget line item entitled, "Innovation Investments." That way innovation becomes a normal part of how you operate your business.*

Brainstorming. This is a no-brainer! But do you do enough of it in an atmosphere that is conducive to the production of bright ideas from everyone in the company? In Chapter 2, Leader Avenue, we talked about using the whole brain of an organization where the sum of the parts is better than any one part and where everyone's input is welcome.

Some key concepts for brainstorming are sharing opportunities such as open discussions, communicating, listening, and feedback, asking for suggestions and new ideas and finding the right catalyst to make things happen. And some healthy friction is fine—it can often be quite productive. As Dorothy Leonard and Susan Straus proclaim in Harvard Business Review's *On Knowledge Management:*

> The manager successful at fostering innovation figures out how to get different approaches to grate against one another in a productive process we call *creative abrasion.*

Imitation. You're a copycat—so what? As long as you do not violate copyrights, patents and ethical business standards, you're fine. It's called keeping up with the latest happenings in an ever-changing world and following trends in your industry.

You aren't the only innovator and don't have all the bright ideas, so take advantage of other innovators in your business and borrow ideas from other industries and apply them to yours. You can even put an old idea to new uses. Imitation can save you a lot of time, energy and money and speed up the innovating process.

Finding a Niche. The innovator seeks out and finds niches—a product or service specialty in your market that nobody else has or doesn't do as well. They are there—all you have to do is take the time and effort to find them.

Short of copyrights and patents, your competition will soon follow you, but it's your niche for a profitable period and you can brag that you are the innovative company that did it first.

Risk. *Take considered and measured risk, not chances.* But remember that it takes a lot of resources of all kinds just to open your doors for business. There is also a major risk— ultimately a larger one—in not innovating. Innovators cannot be afraid of failure, particularly since a series of failures often leads to success. As Lee Iacocca points proclaims:

> The fear of failure brings the fear of taking risks…and you are never going to get what you want out of life without taking some risks. Remember, everything worthwhile carries the risk of failure.

The risks of innovating are the unknowns involved in trying something new and different. Nothing ventured, nothing gained, but the ventured part must be done only after much thought, a cost/benefit projection, and a team consensus.

And so it is your attitude, thinking, practice, brainstorming, imitation, finding a niche, and risk approaches that set the tone in your business for the success or failure of your ability to be creative and instill the art of innovation into your organization. It's great to say you made a lot of money last year, but it's even better to say that new products and services will make your company even more profitable next year.

These seven general guidelines are meant to help you devise specific innovation systems and innovations for your company in your industry. Innovator Avenue is the fast lane, a joy ride and a roller coaster all in one. *Fueled by individual and group creativity, innovation is the engine that pushes businesses to greatness.*

Edison's Electrifying Inventions

Thomas Edison was a very hard worker too and was not satisfied until his inventions—a record 1093 patents—were put to some practical use. He looked at his many technological and financial failures as a path to success and once told a co-worker after some experiments failed, "We haven't failed. We now know a thousand things that won't work, so we're that much closer to finding what will."

Edison, whose son Charles remembered him for his courage, imagination, determination, humility and wit, invented the phonograph, the incandescent light bulb, the microphone, the mimeograph, the medical fluoroscope, the storage battery and the movies. He made the stock ticker, telephone, telegraph and typewriter more commercially feasible. He confirms our definition of innovation as being practical applied creativity.

Mr. Jobs Gets the Job Done Through Innovation

Steven Jobs is a modern day example of persistence in

innovation—one who is never satisfied with having achieved greatness and who continues to build one new idea upon another. He learned early in his career that successful computer companies are always in a state of creative flux.

He and Stephen Wozniak founded Apple computer in 1976 and introduced the Apple I microcomputer that had little commercial value. But the Apple II, a home and small business computer that came out two years later, was an immediate success. In 1983 the Lisa model was the first commercial computer to feature a mouse. Apple introduced the Macintosh, a popular home computer with a graphical user interface (GUI) allowing the user to point to on-screen symbols by clicking a mouse. In 1986 it was the Mac Plus computer and LaserWriter which significantly advanced desktop publishing. Apple replaced the Macintosh with the Power Mac PC in 1994 and successfully introduced the easy to use iMac in 1998.

Jobs was an early proponent of the PC, promoted computers for educational use, and revolutionized the computer industry's hardware and software more than once. He made computers fun, stylish and user friendly. Though his well known ups and downs with Apple and other ventures (he is also CEO of the animated studio Pixar), Steve Jobs has been able to create, innovate and see many of his brilliant ideas through to reality by maintaining a both restless and relentless spirit.

Chapter Five

Manager Avenue

Destination

Unfortunately "management" is a generally overworked catchall term that refers to just about anything to do with running a business. There are many articles, books, courses, and seminars on management and even entire schools offering master degrees in business management. These resources and curricula are meant to provide well-educated business managers.

But in the real business world, actual management functions and responsibilities are only one of five performance avenues. It is not leadership, learning, innovation or promotion. *While leadership, for example, is being effective by doing the right things, management is being efficient by doing things right.* Greater management efficiency produces more with fewer people for customers who demand more for less.

Management is primarily organizational administration and can be broken down into three main areas—*planning, systematizing,* and *directing.* Let's review all three in defining what we do while traveling on Manager Avenue.

Planning

Too often business planning is seen as a boring but necessary evil that is low on the list of priorities. And yet planning can actually be interesting, invigorating and ultimately profitable. A captain charts the course with his crew. *Is a business any different than a ship at sea?*
The benefits of planning include selecting the best course of action from several alternatives, having better control of your future with fewer obstacles and surprises, fostering teamwork in working toward common goals, establishing priorities, allowing for better time management, lowering costs, and increasing profits and setting performance standards for measuring results.
The business planning process starts with interpreting and translating the company's strategy into practical application and proceeds to setting goals and objectives, budgeting, organizing and prioritizing, communicating the plan, and monitoring and adjusting the plan. Implementing the plan will be covered under the systematizing and directing headings later in this chapter.

Interpreting and Translating the Strategy. *There is no such thing as strategic planning!* There is *strategic thinking*, which was discussed in the chapters on Leader Avenue and Innovator Avenue, and its sequel, *business planning.* It's planning that takes the strategy and maps out a course to achieve it.
Interpreting the strategy is learning all about it and then fully understanding it. The strategy can then be translated into the language of management and action. Is the strategy clearly thought through, well defined, and properly interpreted? If so, planning can then begin to develop, break

down and quantify the strategy and formulate what can realistically be accomplished and when.

Goals and Objectives. Goals are the results you and your company are committed to achieving with all of the resources available to you. *You cannot meet a goal that is not set anymore than an archer can hit a target that is not there.* Goals must be clear, concise, worthwhile, realistic, specific, timely, and measurable. And they must be developed by and mutually acceptable to your associates.

Setting goals states your intentions and influences behavior. They indicate to you and everybody else where your company intends to go. And finally, challenging goals test and stretch your abilities to their upper limits.

Objectives are the specifics of what, how, when and at what cost things must be done in order to meet your goals. If, for example, you set a goal to increasing net profits after taxes by 10% next year, you need a list of objectives or actual ways as to how you are going to achieve that goal.

Budgeting. While your annual budget makes you think about employee and operational efficiency, compensation levels and resource allocation, *do not mistake your budget for your business plan.* Your plan is the result of the work you have done *before* you prepare your budget.

Budgeting does give you an opportunity to review each line item to see if its expenditure is justified again for another year. *Zero-based budgeting* and similar systems put all spending through a rigorous annual testing period so that only the necessary and best programs survive. *Flex-budgeting* changes the budget each month based on actual year-to-date experience and revised year-end projections.

Organizing and Prioritizing. Managers are organized. Everything is in order and follows a logical consistent sequence from point A to point B. Start with your desk, then organize your calendar, staff, operations—not to mention the rest of your personal and professional life. Prioritize—that is, simply put first things first. What is most urgent and/or important in terms of time, energy and other resources? *The time you take to prioritize may be your most productive.* Does it help to put things off that are time consuming, difficult or unpopular?

Communicating the Plan. What good is a plan if your associates either don't know what it is or don't have a clear understanding of it? The plan needs to be a well written one that also has a summary of its major parts.

Present the plan appropriately to all of your stakeholders including with your employees, stockholders, business associates, customers, and the general public. This sets the level of expectation and gets everyone moving in the same direction towards the company's stated goals.

Monitoring and Adjusting the Plan. Something must be accurately measured before it can be properly analyzed. So the elements of the business plan from activity reports to financial statements must be quantified in a way that results can be posted against projections. A quarterly review of your plan will indicate whether or not you are on track, what problems you may be encountering and who is accountable for what went right or wrong.

Plan on adjusting the plan periodically, especially before it's too late. Things happen that are beyond your control and new information can change your thinking and cause you to re-evaluate your plan.

Systematizing

One of the most important but often overlooked things

that a good manager does is to devise and implement management systems throughout their sphere of influence. *A management system is a network of interrelated procedures that organizes and channels a group of activities into a specified and consistent chain of events.* There is order and efficiency with systems and chaos and waste without them.

With the right management systems a company can virtually run itself. Delegation is streamlined and everybody works more autonomously. Your people are not mind readers—they need and want what to know what to do and how to do it. They tend to think their system is best unless they are persuaded otherwise. Do you want everybody guessing about what they should do and operating on their own individual systems?

The best management systems are developed both from the top of the organizational chart and from the grass roots of the company as well as, in some cases, feedback from your customers. *Those operating within a system must help create it, buy into it and partner with it.* Checks and balances are effective management tools to look for potential problems and avoid costly mistakes, but can only be deployed where there is regularity that is derived from well-defined systems.

There is a system for all company functions whether defined or not. Systems go from the simple to the complex and from the informal to the formal. But they must forever be fluid and flexible and be prepared to react to constant changes and enhancements.

After we have made our business plan and installed the management systems to implement the plan, let's see what the "manager-director" does to pull it all together.

Directing

The proactive busy job of a director calling the shots on a movie set pretty well sums up what it is like to be on Manager Avenue. After the planning and systematizing are completed, the director is heavily involved in a whole gamut of action-oriented management functions we will call *directing*. It definitely has men and women in business test-driving through some rough terrain.

Directing is the *doing* after all the *thinking*—it actually implements the business plan and installs the management systems. Directing has five distinct yet related parts—*decision-making, problem solving, interacting, empowerment and getting results.*

Decision-making. As we indicated in Chapter Three, decision-making is simply making smart choices from as many alternatives as possible. A decision is no better than the best alternative looked at. Preparation is the key and that is why we need to spend enough time on Learner Avenue. *Good decision makers have a deep knowledge reservoir and are always studying their options.*

And objectivity must take precedent over emotion, impatience, and impulsiveness. We also must know how our personality type underlies our approaches to decision making. For example, are you prone to make decisions too quickly in order to get the matter settled before carefully considering all the alternatives?

Decisions and their effects need to be projected to see which short- and long-term consequences that are mostly likely to result from a certain decision. *A decision cannot be made in isolation, particularly since each decision leads to another one in a long decision chain.*

You can read lots of books on decision making, figure out how to use a "decision tree" and/or as I suggest, try the "yellow pad feedback method". Whenever you have an important decision to make, take a yellow pad, propose a decision, draw a line down the middle of a sheet of paper, and put the positive things on left side and the negative things on the right side. Then write out your final decision at the bottom of the page. Confirm and possibly modify your decision by asking the advice and opinion of one or two other people. It's easy to do and it makes you think, struggle and seek the best decision.

Problem Solving. Problem solving—often called meeting a challenge—is an offspring of its kin decision-making. It is often needed to adjust or correct a management decision or deal with new circumstances beyond anyone's control.

The first step in the problem solving process is creating a corporate culture that recognizes there are in fact always some problems to solve. No sweeping them under the rug allowed. The second step is gathering all available information about the problem and clearly and completely defining it.

Now you are ready to offer solutions—don't just go for the first one you think about or solve it the way you always have in the past. Consider cost, time, human resources and other relevant factors and work through the scenarios of several ways of meeting the challenge. Pick the best one, test it and put it into place. Don't let obstacles hold you back and don't give up without a fight.

Interacting. Most managers are interacting with people all day long and their people skills will make or break them. The importance of socializing discussed in the Chapter Two, Leader Avenue, holds true for Manager Avenue as well.

Your dominant style of communicating can be crucial to your success at interacting. Consider one that is on the informal side. Tom Peters and Robert Waterman discuss informality and Management By Walking About (MBWA) in *In Search of Excellence* and assert, "Whether it's their rich ways of communicating informally or their special ways of using ad hoc devices, such as task forces, the excellent companies get quick action just because their organizations are fluid."

Interacting takes in a whole host of physical and psychological areas of human behavior including body language, gesturing, face reading, communicating, and emotions of all kinds. It includes questioning, listening, speaking, cajoling, mediating, thanking, encouraging, writing, presenting, instructing, and counseling. The manager cannot be all things to all people, but is constantly asked to be.

It is a big help to be aware of your own personality type, thinking style, temperament, attitude, and background as well as that of the person you are interacting with. And you need to understand first and then to be understood. Successful interacting takes an active, assertive approach to all the forms of communication involved. *It's hard work!*

Empowerment. You can do a lot yourself, but you can't do it all. So if you are going to grow your business at all, you need to hire, train, and develop the best people you can find. *Companies are no more successful on a long-term basis than the people who work for them.*

Hiring the right people is such a constant challenge that managers sometimes try to take shortcuts, hire too quickly without enough due diligence, and often suffer serious consequences. Good employees make a manager's job easy, bad ones make life miserable. Human resources are your main resources and deserve your main attention.

Effective empowerment leads everyone to their highest potential and involves hiring, proper placement, orienting, instructing, teaching, training, supporting, correcting, disciplining, motivating, promoting, and rewarding. They need to know what their job is, what their performance expectations are, and to be delegated the right amount of responsibility and the authority to go with it. All associates in any organization should readily be able to answer the question, *"What do I get paid to do?"*

Getting Results. In the final analysis, it is measurable results that count. Before you claim that it is only the financial bottom line that matters, think about results in a bigger picture that includes the success of your people themselves and how your company has improved your industry and positively impacted society.

Empowered employees will get results, but to the extent your established company management systems allow, let them do it their way. *The best approach is outcome-based management with results having priority over methods and the end being more important than the means.* It's getting there without prescribing exactly how. Give your people enough space and let them be innovators—continuous and contemporary improvers—as to how they achieve or exceed targeted goals.

Directions

We have defined organizational management in a nutshell and described what good managers do. In the following Directions section let's take a closer look at how to reach Performance Peak by building on what you have already achieved and being the best manger you can be. We have provided a discussion entitled "Under All Managers," created the Manager's Field Guide that lists 25 of the most effective and efficient management directives for immediate application in your work environment, and added concepts related to enhancing your management skills.

Under All Managers

In examining how to be a great manager, let's reflect on how well you have developed your management skills to date and your underlying motivational and support systems in three ways—*preparation*, *drive*, *simplicity* and *alliances*.

Preparation. There are many stops on Learner Avenue for the aspiring manager including academic centers, basic training camps, experience trails and the School of Hard Knocks. How well we take advantage of each learning opportunity is critical to our long-term success as a manager. Moreover, learning about the subjective and intangible areas of life rounds out our more objective knowledge. Understanding, for example, that there is no substitute for hard work and the value of business ethics, helps prepare you to successfully meet the management challenge. Knowing that you never actually graduate from the School of Hard Knocks is humbling, but part of the realization that you are always preparing for the next level of management.

Drive. Drive is something that we are born with and that is nurtured over time. Deep down, it involves our reason for being and our purpose in life. It's why we get up in the morning.

We have discussed leaders and managers motivating others to achieve their peak performance. It is equally important that we be sure that we keep our own motivation up to speed. *When you start feeling bored, tired, burnt out, or disinterested with what you are doing, it's important to find out why and make some adjustments.* Turning on to Innovator Avenue and thinking new thoughts for a while often helps.

Simplicity. Simplicity is an important management approach that disciplines the manager to communicate with the fewest words and act through the shortest circuits possible. Time, conciseness and directness are always of the essence in managing others and result in "hitting the nail in the head" while avoiding "beating around the bush." John Scully of Apple Computer fame once observed, "Everything we have learned in the industrial age has tended to create more and more complication. I think that more and more people are learning that you have to simplify, not complicate. Simplicity is the ultimate sophistication." Keep it simple.

Alliances. Alliances are the connecting bridges that form partnerships throughout the long journey of your career and support the managers in carrying out their responsibilities. We all need friends in business and "a friend in need is a friend indeed."

Since all managers have shortcomings, they need partners to shore them up and add strength where they are weak. A network of partners, friends and associates both inside and outside of a company adds real value to any manager by broadening his or her stability, scope and sphere of influence.

Manager's Field Guide
The Top Twenty-Five

1) Know thyself—self knowledge underlies all you do.
2) Do not live in denial of anything—ever.
3) Communicate and understand well—always.
4) Be objective more than emotional and influence others with values, facts, logic and reason.
5) Check your ego and exercise more humility and humor.
6) Admit your mistakes quickly and emphatically.
7) Build relationships with your associates and if there is a conflict, resolve it quickly.
8) Make people stronger rather than weaker.
9) Work in teams with lots of energy and synergy.
10) Hire and keep the best people in your industry.

11) Do not surround yourself with "yes" people.
12) Do not promote someone beyond both your practical and emotional intelligence.
13) Be sure everybody knows what they get paid to do.
14) Buy right and help your vendors become more efficient.
15) Do first things first and don't procrastinate.
16) Understand the company's strategy and direction.
17) Allocate your resources to what is most profitable.
18) Follow your business plan, but plan on changing it.
19) Remember that your annual budget is not your plan.
20) There is a system for everything.
21) Look at lots of alternatives and make smart choices.
22) It's the outcome more than how you get there—results over method and the end over the means.
23) Don't criticize the competition, but watch your back.
24) Run scared—good companies can go bad.
25) If somebody else in your company can do something better than you, let them do it.

Enhancement Approaches

Your management skills are enhanced slowly but surely—step by step. And that's fine since you will not become a markedly improved manager overnight. Keep the learning curve vertical with experience, reading, education, and imitation of good managers. And get some honest feedback from others on how you are doing.

Being a better manager is experimental—by trial and error. When you find you are getting it right, continue in the same direction and when getting it wrong, try something else. Become familiar with proven management principles and systems and practice applying them to your organization.

If, for example, you identify problems with your organizing or people skills or your personality, work on improving them, but also delegate things you do not do well to somebody else. No manager is perfect.

It is particularly hard to get to Performance Peak and be the best you can be without being a good manager, a skill that often does not come easily. Set some management skill level goals for yourself and make a list of objectives on how to reach those goals. Spend whatever time you need to on Manager Avenue.

In conclusion, management is about planning and expediting the plan. It's the nuts and bolts of getting the job done in a prioritized, organized, and efficient way. *Managers make the products and provide the services after the leaders, learners and innovators have set the strategy, know what to do and have come up with the best ideas.*

General Eisenhower, Supreme Allied Manager

In January 1944 General Dwight Eisenhower became the Supreme Allied Commander of the forces that were to invade the European mainland somewhere along the coast at Normandy in what was known as "Operation Overlord." The Allies faced Hitler's fearsome "Atlantic Wall" of fortifications, mines and obstacles, some of which were underwater, as well as massive German land, air and sea power. After deceiving Hitler into believing the invasion would take place further to the northeast in Pas-de-Calais and bombing count-less French bridges, the allies struck Normandy with a vast armada of airplanes, ships and landing craft from the south of England on June 6, 1944—the D-day invasion that was depicted so vividly in the film *Saving Private Ryan.*

After listening to Churchill elevate this coming event as a probable hinge of history by saying, "I have confidence in you my commanders. The fate of the world is in your hands," Eisenhower focused on the final two months of preparation for D-day. The staggering logistics of this mili-tary operation alone—without modern computers—are hard to imagine. Eisenhower was up to the task at hand—he and his staff worked the plan, installed the systems, solved the problems, and directed the action. It was Eisenhower's tac-tical expertise, decisiveness, likeability, and ability to empower others that secured an outcome-based result—the right outcome.

Sam's Rules

Wal-Mart's founder Sam Walton wrote a book that stated these ten "Rules for Building a Business" which he said worked for him and involved simple common sense:

1. COMMIT to your business.
2. SHARE your profits with all your associates, and treat them as partners.
3. MOTIVATE your partners.
4. COMMUNICATE everything you possibly can to your partners.
5. APPRECIATE everything your associates do for the business.
6. CELEBRATE your success.
7. LISTEN to everyone in your company.
8. EXCEED your customers' expectations.

9. CONTROL your expenses better than your competition.
10. SWIM upstream.

Walton, who grew up on a Missouri farm to become the richest man in America, had an extraordinarily keen sense of what it is to consistently manage well. He stuck with his rules and did indeed build a business that is the benchmark of management principles for retailing and, in fact, every other business that sells a product. From his first store in 1945 to the giant chain it has become, Sam Walton had a system that he simply repeated over and over in small towns across America. He changed the way we shop—and the way we manage.

Chapter Six

Promoter Avenue

Destination

Now that you are a leader, learner, innovator and manager, the only remaining thing you need to be is a promoter. Being a promoter is basically marketing and selling all your knowledge, skills and products and all that your have to offer the world—to everyone you come in contact with both inside and outside of your organization.

Yes, the promoter is a salesperson, but he or she is much more that that. They are observers, explainers, and influencers. Without being a good promoter, the four other performance avenues you travel on are not nearly as effective as they could be. For example, what if you have a great idea but it is poorly packaged or are a gifted leader but do nor express yourself well?

In this Destination section, we are going to define promotion and the promoter answering these three simple questions:

- *What is promotion and what does a promoter do?*

- *Who should you be promoting to?*
- *Why promote yourself and your business?*

As usual the "how" to promote will be covered under the Directions section to follow.

What?

The three P's of promotion are *perception, presentation* and *persuasion*. We will define these three concepts and see how they are related.

Perception. You have heard the expression "perception is everything." For promotion, perception is first being in touch with your customers and knowing why and how they make their buying decisions. And secondly, it is your corporate image and your brand name—that is, how your customers consistently perceive your company and its products and services. On a personal level, promotion involves how you perceive your people and how they perceive you. *Perception is a two-way street.*

The biggest problem, of course, arises when perceptions are wrong for any number of reasons. Promoters must know their audience to be effective. It is also their job to be sure that the way in which something is promoted results in an honest and realistic perception.

Presentation. The heart of promotion lies in the way something is presented. This covers the art and science—the psychology really—of both individual and corporate advertising, marketing and selling. It involves how information is presented and received. For example, is the presentation targeted, clear, concise, interesting, exciting, timely, and friendly? To what extent are each of the five senses involved? Whether an idea, a service or a product—

is it well packaged?

Both your intended and unintended presentations form a continuous promotional stream and both lead to how you are perceived. It's just when you think that you are not being recorded that the microphone is still on.

Persuasion. The purpose of any presentation is to persuade, influence, convince, convict, and ultimately to transform. It's Phase III of the "Learning Ladder" that we discussed in Chapter Three, Learner Avenue. Persuasion starts with defining exactly what it is you are promoting followed by basic education—explaining, instructing, teaching, and training—of those minds you want to change and to conform to yours.

Negotiation is a form of persuasion that often entails finding out where someone is on a particular issue and getting them from there to your point of view. It also involves objectively convincing them that believing in and agreeing with what you are offering will cause them to be more fulfilled and successful. And according to the bestseller *Getting to Yes* by Roger Fisher and William Ury, successful negotiating involves focusing each other's specific interests rather than both sides digging in with hardened positions.

Negotiating is coming up with mutually acceptable options and win/win solutions that meet with the approval of the one being persuaded. But remember as Steve Covey points out in *The Seven Habits of Highly Effective People*— a synergistic solution should be *win/win or no deal*—that is, agree or agree to disagree for now.

Persuasion is also about creating a legitimate desire by demonstrating a need or want along with a way to satisfy that desire. Advertisers are experts at this form of persuasion, but we all need to understand the desire-need-want-satisfaction formula for changing someone's mind. It is a matter of obtaining well-interpreted survey information, being aware of social and fashion trends and shifts in buying habits, and the psychology of the buyer you are pursuing.

Who?

In an individual sense, since you are, one way or another, always promoting something, everybody you come in contact with is a client or customer of some kind. In business it is critical to determine who exactly is your customer. You must ask, "Who do I market and sell to?" This selection process has to do with matching your products and services with the right buyer who is willing to pay the right price. It's about marketing research and prospecting that identifies people who need and want what you have to offer and, in addition, provides them with a good reason and a convenient way to buy it.

When the who to promote to becomes the who to do business with, promotion becomes centered on business relationships. This client partnering then finds areas of mutual advantage to solidify the reasons to do business together. And then, according to Larry Wilson in *Stop Selling, Start Partnering*, it's *partnering* rather than *selling*.

Why?

The primary reason to promote is to communicate and set a level of expectation. People do not really know how great your ideas or your products and services are unless you demonstrate it to them. Moreover, the listener, be it one of your own associates or your customers, may have to overcome some concerns and objections in order to be convinced to buy an idea, product or service. *For a customer, the right kind of promotion achieves a comfort level that validates their decision.*

This comfort level is further enhanced by promotion that

includes a contagious enthusiasm. You show your customers how much you like something and they will like it too.

Promotion is not only done to win over new converts and customers, but to keep the ones you have. All companies need repeat business in the form of customers who buy again and tell others to buy too—what might be called a *word-of-mouth referral network*. It's innovative and effective promotion of all kinds that helps maintain a high degree of excitement and brand loyalty.

Directions

Promotion of yourself is not done by just one part of you, but by all parts—that is, a holistic approach with all you say and do. And promotion of your business is not done by just the sales and marketing department, but by everybody in the company and all that they do. It is your total package, your entire image and the sum of your cumulative advertising all in one. *Promotion is the way a company talks.*

Promotion begins with *the message* you need and want to communicate, how *the messenger* promotes the message, and *the reply*, that is, the response from the customer's viewpoint that puts you in their shoes. The right message delivered in the right way to the right people will produce a positive reply.

The Message

Promotional messages are basically the personal and corporate images that you want to project. This process for your company starts on Leader Avenue with visioning, a mission statement and your strategy.

This message must be complete and include everything a customer sees, hears and otherwise comes in contact with regarding anything to do with your business. All of your image building, advertising, goodwill, and promotional activities must be consistent and project the same theme about your company.

And the promotional message must dovetail with your marketing research on buyer behavior and decision making to be effective. What can you tell your customers about your product and services that causes them to buy? What is most important to them? What do they value most and how can what you offer be of value to them?

In this world of bytes and bits, all messages have to be short and to the point and hit the customer's "hot buttons" immediately. *Whatever the customer can remember and hold in their conscious memory is critical.* That's why memorable credos, logos and ads are so effective. Who, for example, earns your business the old fashioned way? Smith Barney, of course.

The more subjective and subtle side of promotion should not be overlooked. Those intangibles such as trust, integrity, and reliability are biggies. You could, for example, emphasize that your company is your #1 product or that you are customer-oriented and reserve the right to exceed your customer's expectations.

The message should not over-promise, but it must present your business in its best possible light. For example, you are not just selling a product or service as Joseph Pine and James Gilmore state in *The Experience Economy*, but also providing a *great experience* for your customers—and they should know that.

The message must further emphasize what makes you different and sets you apart in the marketplace and what is new and exciting about what you are promoting. Domino's Pizza has been a huge success for one main reason—it became known not for the quality of its pizza, but for fast (within 30 minutes) delivery. When Apple Computer came up with the concept of a "personal" computer, sales soared.

Finally, there are two key points to remember that are too often overlooked. *Products and services are sold, not bought*—customers must be given a good reason to buy. And closely related to that, *customers need to be asked to buy*— an attractively packaged invitation goes a long way. Effective messages stick to doing both of these things, whether directly or indirectly. It's like the politician saying, "My plans for the future are the best ones. I ask for your vote."

The Messenger

You (that is, you, your people and your company) are the message! The way your company communicates and the way in which a promotional message is delivered are as important as the message itself. You are the storyteller, the evangelist, and the politician all in one and so are all the messengers you send out with the message.

The messenger must deliver a short but complete message. At the very least, their message must briefly describe themselves, their company, their products and services, their customers and their record and reputation. *You have one chance to make a great first impression and many* other *chances to make a lasting one.* Be positive and don't criticize your competition.

It is also up to the messenger to do some serious *showcasing, spotlighting,* and *sizzling.* Take the really important and exciting stuff you want to promote and put it in a case, shine a light on it and let it sizzle. And do it in a way that builds this excitement and keeps the buyers' attention focused on the best aspects of your product.

The messenger balances and blends the visual and audio senses as well as all the modern technological media available today. Packaging with words, images, color, sounds, and songs combine to inform, create desire, invite, demonstrate value, and capture. The message hits home. And to keep it hitting home, we can add another "P" to promotion—*perseverance*. The winning messenger, energized by the message, perseveres under all circumstances.

In all their endeavors the messenger raises to a higher level and is much more successful when seen as what they really are or should be—a consultant, counselor, advisor, and helper, even a friend, rather than purely as a sales representative. *When salespeople are perceived as educated and experienced professionals in their field, their clients have much more confidence in them.* That's why terms such as "sales consultant" or "account executive" can be helpful and why so many companies have a "vice-president" handling your sales account.

But it is also the little things that can become big things for the messenger who is promoting a message. Marriott's success in the hotel business can be attributed in part to its training of its employees most of whom who are, after all, Marriott's primary messengers to the public. They are given a wallet card to remind them of six disciplined behaviors not to be violated:

1. Smile and greet every guest.
2. Speak to the quest in a warm, friendly courteous manner.
3. Display a genuine and enthusiastic interest.
4. Anticipate guest needs and be flexible in responding to them.
5. Be knowledgeable about your job.
6. Learn to take ownership of guest problems and resolve them.

From little things to big things the messenger's job is never over. And the message and the messenger are delivered together at the same time.

The Reply

We discussed interacting in the previous chapter, Manager Avenue. The same principles hold true for Promoter Avenue. Promotion is constant interaction with your listeners and customers and, as we said earlier in this chapter, is a two-way street. Promotion is like a reflected beam of light—you send it out from a source of light and look for its return. You have to know if your message is getting across effectively.

There needs to be some kind of formal and/or informal survey and information gathering done to test customer reaction to both your products and services and how well you are promoting them. Is customer reaction positive or negative and how so? Is there a problem with the message or the messenger? You may think you are the greatest promoter in the world, but do your customers agree? When my home-building company did a customer survey, 90% of our customers said they would recommend our company to someone else which is a very high statistic in the building industry. But we learned a lot form the other 10%!

Ever listen to the pundits critique a political speech? Try some of their methods to analyze your own speeches and other communications. Role-play and practice selling and negotiating. Be your own best critic. But also get loads of feedback of all kinds from your customers. Do they perceive a consistent quality image-building program? Are they satisfied customers? Are they becoming enthusiastic converts? What is their input on what you can do to improve?

In *Direct From Dell, Strategies That Revolutionized an Industry*, Michael Dell reminds us to:

> Think about the customer, not the competition: Competitors represent your industry's past, as, over the years, collective habits become ingrained. Customers

are your future, representing new opportunities, ideas, and avenues for growth.

Jack Welch of General Electric is known for saying, "Everything we do is aimed at either getting a customer or keeping a customer." Go out of your way to stay in touch with your customers at all times. They are a moving target and you have to know where they are going to keep one step ahead of them.

In conclusion, being a promoter is about focusing a sharp, memorable and influential message and effectively presenting it to a well defined and targeted customer base. It's asking and getting them to buy, feeling good about their purchase and developing brand loyalty. Promotion is crucial to everything else you do. As someone once said, "Doing business without advertising is like winking in the dark. You know what you are doing, but nobody else does."

And keep in mind that anyone can be a great promoter. Three stonemasons were once asked what they were doing. One said that he was a laborer hauling rocks and another one that he was an artisan creating beautiful stonework. But the third one said that he was a master builder constructing a magnificent cathedral!

Robert Woodruff, Coca-Cola Salesman

Dr. J.S. Pemberton, a formulator of medicines in Atlanta, invented a very satisfying soft drink in 1886. Robert Woodruff presided over the impressive growth of the Coca-Cola empire for the sixty years following his father's purchase of the company in 1919. World War II allowed Coca-Cola to conquer the globe and it was rationed at home during the war so that soldiers overseas could have it. Woodruff died two months before Coke briefly changed its formula in 1985.

He believed that selling and salespeople were every bit as important as innovation and production. Woodruff passionately explains here, in part, what it is to be a salesman in his book, *You in a Career of Selling*:

> The salesman's personal integrity, his belief in himself and his product must be an essential part of each sales agreement, if the company selling and the customer buying are mutually to benefit….He cannot really separate himself from his product, even after he has sold it and delivery has been effected….
>
> No historian has truly told the story of the salesman in the rapid development and productive growth of our country. The soldier, the statesmen, the pioneer, the Indian fighter have all had their biographers. The salesman played an equally important role. He moved goods along the rivers and trails. The men who went into the frontier with goods to exchange for furs, the traders who opened trading posts deep in the wilderness—all these were part of a necessary movement and distribution of consumer goods and products. "Selling" was then, as now, the motive power in our prosperity and growth….
>
> We tend to think of the Industrial Revolution in terms of vast new machines, of automation, of mass production and assembly. But nothing happens until a salesman books an order.

Ronald Reagan, the Great Communicator

We mentioned President Ronald Reagan earlier in this chapter. His exceptional ability to present a message was his means not only of getting to the White House, but also into the history books as one of the most effective communicators of all time. His background as an actor and Governor of

California enhanced his natural gifts as a messenger who could promote a message and take it to its highest potential.

On the international scene, for example, Reagan put a chilling effect on the Cold War, not just by stating and restating America's position of peace through strength and labeling Russia as an "evil empire," but with the power of his unmatched charm, wit, and vigor that gave him a decided and sustained competitive advantage in an ugly ongoing fight to the finish. I vividly remember watching the evening news when he stood in front of the Berlin Wall and challenged his archenemy with this one-liner, "Mr. Gorbachov, tear down this wall!" Ronald Reagan was a winning, even prophetic, messenger—and he was instrumental in winning the Cold War for his country.

Chapter Seven

Performance Types

In this chapter we will deal with our two most often used avenues that are like two streets meeting at an intersection. There are ten such distinct intersections where one performance avenue meets another one and forms a performance type.

Your performance type is a combination of your two most dominant avenues that best describe and define your approach to conducting your affairs and operating at work. This does not mean that you do not have other strengths and travel on the other three less dominant avenues, but that most of your time is naturally spent on these two.

Review these performance types and get familiar with them. You will then be in a position to take the performance test in the next chapter. As with other behavior tests such as Myers-Briggs, the descriptions of each type are not be an exact one for everybody with that type, but are generally quite close and very useful. After you have determined your type via the performance test, go back over the description of your type, see how close it is, and adjust it with all the additional knowledge you have about yourself.

This book is meant to help you analyze how both your strengths and weakness affect your decision-making and behavior. Determining and understanding your performance type is all about self-awareness and gradual shifts in your thinking followed by some positive behavioral modifications and performance improvement.

Performance types can be used in some of the same ways psychological types are used in the area of human resources and management—in hiring, personnel evaluation, position assignments, promotions, assessment of the mix of performance types on a team, decision making, and problem solving. Performance types provide a system for knowing who is best at what tasks from an actual operational perspective that can predict how people will function in their work environment in terms of their performance comfort zone. This typing is also a diagnostic tool for determining how to better train people to understand and improve themselves and how to better understand and work together with others.

We will review each one of these types and demonstrate the potential strengths ("Passing Lanes") and potential challenges ("Detours") of each type. We have also provided an "Are likely to" prediction of some of the most likely results of the decisions and action that characterize a particular performance type.

Leader-Managers

Passing Lanes: Have insightful vision; inspiring; top strategist; in full command and control; know what's going on; well organized; prioritize; confident; passionate; fearless; popular; great by-the-book coaches.

Detours: Know-it-alls; feel invincible; don't always keep up with the times; skeptical about new ideas; not concerned enough about perceptions; have some difficulty in communicating the message.

Are likely to: Assertively run a business; do well in an organized setting such as the military; find people to do what they are not good at; learn only what that have to; chair great meetings; know and execute strong motivational programs; have clear five year business plans in place; build successful teams that operate on their own; form strong business alliances.

Innovator-Promoters

Passing Lanes: Optimistic dreamers; energized by engaging the chaos and bright ideas; see possibilities others do not; tell the story enthusiastically; unconventional persuaders.

Detours: Lack overall strategy; not big on research; can be impractical and disorganized; not systems-oriented; weak on delegating; get upset with criticism.

Are likely to: Come up with new products that will sell well; tackle unpopular problems and then brag about solving them; promote an idea that they may have not thoroughly researched themselves; help others promote their innovations.

Learner-Leaders

Passing Lanes: Convicted; committed; have a clear big picture of the future; learn from mistakes; listen to customers; know the competition, teachers; trainers; set an expectation level.

Detours: Prefer the status quo; wary of new concepts; do not prioritize well; personal interaction is a problem; micro-manage at times; message is too long; presentations are sometimes too detailed.

Are likely to: Be very comfortable with being leaders of companies or teams within a company; be critical of others' leadership ability; analyze their own leadership qualities and learn from experience; understand people and how to get the best out of them; take conservative business risks rather than unwise chances; have great difficulty stepping down from their position or retiring.

Promoter-Managers

Passing Lanes: Perceptive; decides quickly and openly; organized presenter; friendly; win others over to a plan; empower people; get expected results and brag about them.

Detours: Experience some knowledge gaps; can miss the big picture; do not appreciate creativity enough; promote business as usual; don't vary the routine or rock the boat.

Are likely to: Be perfect sales managers; hire the best sales people and train them well by-the-book; know what the customer wants; always have a marketing plan and budget; need help in looking for new markets; be better employees than business owners; look more at sales results than methods; put in long hours; dress well and look good at all times; answer all phone calls enthusiastically.

Learner-Innovators

Passing Lanes: Want to know and understand how everything works; deep thinkers; believe in conservative change; exercise wisdom; energized by knowledge that leads to new and useful improvements.

Detours: Self- rather than company-motivated; keep too much to themselves; always trying to change the system; assume their listeners are knowledgeable; don't find enough time for promotional activities.

Are likely to: Want to comment on everything and not be left out; be very effective staff members; be excellent consultants and counselors; come up with well thought out new policies; have difficulty with leadership and management roles; stay in their offices; be insightful authors of business books; make great research scientists.

Leader-Promoters

Passing Lanes: Great communicators; magnetic persuaders; global thinkers with a grand vision; excellent social skills; have avid followers; accept feedback; superior selling ability.

Detours: Can be poorly prepared; don't go much beyond one-liners; new ideas are usually not theirs'; systems and efficiency are for somebody else to worry about.

Are likely to: Be winning and effective politicians and business leaders; meet challenges with a can-do attitude; realize their shortcomings and delegate around them; listen to their subordinates and tell them how to get the job done; focus on promotion not innovation for business growth.

Manager-Innovators

Passing Lanes: Plan on changing the plan; systematize the creative process; use innovative business management tools; mission oriented; emphasize outcome-based results.

Detours: Alter the vision and strategy at times; don't coach by the book; don't care what you think of them; too preoccupied to really listen and learn; believe ideas should sell themselves.

Are likely to: Think through the steps needed to develop new products and services; become frustrated by having to change directions toward what they believe is a better idea; independent but prioritized innovators; empower people by giving them good ideas; not afraid of well organized paradigm shifts; make great R & D heads.

Promoter-Learners

Passing Lanes: Spirited self-confident speakers; develop and know the message well; evangelists for what is right; interact by exchanging information; wisdom brokers.

Detours: Don't look to the future; won't subordinate their own agenda; picky; bothered by the chaos of innovation; define the problem; but have trouble solving it.

Are likely to: Keep their office open so they can tell you what they know and what you need to know; have good arguments but often push them too hard; be good staff people who are glad to support leaders, innovators and managers; benchmark well and are more comfortable promoting proven ideas than new ones; be great customer surveyors; admit their mistakes so others don't repeat them.

Innovator-Leaders

Passing Lanes: Positive attitude; think globally; stay on the cutting edge; like to be first; entrepreneurs; network well; get others excited about new ventures; persevere.

Detours: Take too much unmeasured risk; speak without knowing all the facts; impulsive at times; can be dictatorial; don't work well with established systems; somewhat undisciplined messengers.

Are likely to: Take a business to great heights; usually way ahead of the pack; listen intently to other innovators on the team; struggles with subordinating their own agenda; always have blockbuster management retreats; like to create one paradigm after another—needed or not; shoot from the hip; strategize more than plan; have too little fear of failure; find new ways to motivate employees.

Manager-Learners

Passing Lanes: Accumulate and apply practical knowledge; reason well; problem solvers; detailed planners; strict budgeters; understand people; measure results well.

Detours: Overly conservative; procrastinate; can be shortsighted; rely on the past and are threatened by change; reluctant messengers; inflexible.

Are likely to: Have the best education and training programs; have the most organized R & D departments; learn a lot from their mistakes; study their options endlessly; interact well with learners; over analyze monthly statements; criticize reports for being too short; win an argument; be well prepared for meetings; read this book.

There you have it. A new way of looking at how you and your associates perform at work. Don't worry about which avenue was listed first. It's your two most dominant avenues and are okay being listed either way. For example, either Manager-Learner or Learner-Manager is fine—performance types are an art as well as a science. But if someone is actually a manager, you might be more comfortable saying Learner-Manager and if a leader, Innovator-Leader and so on.

And the content of the *Passing Lanes*, *Detours* and *Are likely to* sections can be supplemented by your own evaluation of yourself, your experiences, and the work environment and unique circumstances of your company. What we have provided here is a framework and further development within that framework is encouraged and may be necessary for more fully understanding someone's performance type. One way to do that is to review the chapters of each of the two avenues in question and see how these avenues interact and predict how that particular type will usually perform. The Appendix in the back of this book provides a brief summarized outline of each performance avenue as a handy reference.

The Meeting

Now let's apply the concept of performance types to a hypothetical meeting of ten people—one of each of the ten performance types. We will have them each say a few words that are consistent with their type to better illustrate what we actually mean by a performance type and how useful this concept can be in the critical area of understanding people.

Leader-Manager. "I would like to share with everybody the preliminary outline of our latest corporate strategy and vision for the future. Here is a handout with the seven major initiatives clearly spelled out. I'd like to go around the room and get a brief comment from each of you."

Innovator-Promoter. "I'm real excited and am sure this will be a huge success. The brighter the ideas, the better! But it's also the perception of it that will be crucial to its success."

Learner-Leader. "I hope this outline contains some real meat on the bones that we can all become committed to. Have we learned all we can from our past mistakes?"

Promoter-Manager: "I'm sure we can get the whole company behind this outline if we present it right. Let's do it in a prioritized way this time."

Learner-Innovator. "I can support a final report that has enough imagination and detail. And let's not leave any stones unturned and do some real old-fashioned brainstorming."

Leader-Promoter. "We need a new strategy that will be a true paradigm shift and keep us way ahead of the competition. I'm sure somebody in this room has the right answer. It's really a no-brainer!"

Manager-Innovator. "But let's keep the plan flexible, you know, kind of fluid—strategies have a way of changing with new ideas. Besides, it's really the end, not the means that's important."

Promoter-Learner. "Let's keep everything in this room until we know exactly what we are talking about. Actually, I'm more comfortable with touching up our current strategy—our problem has been poor marketing."

Innovator-Leader. "Look, we have to step up to the plate here and push the envelope. It's obvious to me that we are holding back—entrepreneurs take risks to succeed. We have to do whatever it takes to stay on the cutting edge."

Manager-Learner. "Yes, but we absolutely have to get our ducks in a row first. No doubt, this is the first of many drafts of this strategy outline—with a ton of homework to do. Calm down, we'll eventually get to the right answer."

Leader-Manager. "I want to thank all of you for those comments—I'm sure that with everybody's input, we can build a consensus here and make the smartest choices. Now we're going to spend the next 15 minutes discussing initiative #1."

Is it a little clearer where we are going now? The point is that there were ten responses to the same question. We are defining and analyzing here what you have observed in similar meetings for years. And we are trying to get a better understanding of ourselves and other people and how everyone performs at work.

Examples

First we return to Ronald Reagan—this time as the clear and notable example of a performance type. President Reagan is a Leader-Promoter. His leadership qualities are as legendary as Abraham Lincoln's, and as we mentioned earlier, he is one of the best promoters in recent history. Promoter Avenue is his most dominant performance avenue and Leader Avenue his secondary one. His narrower avenues are Learner Avenue—he did not do a lot of his own research of the issues; Innovator Avenue—many of the ideas he promoted where not his own original ones; and Manager Avenue—he admittedly was a mediocre manager and wisely delegated management functions to others. Other modern American Presidents and their performance types are:

Franklin Roosevelt – Innovator-Leader
Harry Truman – Promoter-Leader
Dwight Eisenhower – Leaner-Manager
John Kennedy – Promoter-Leader
Lyndon Johnson – Promoter-Leader
Richard Nixon – Learner-Manager
Gerald Ford – Leader-Manager
Jimmy Carter – Learner-Innovator
George Bush – Manager-Leader
Bill Clinton – Promoter-Leader
George W. Bush – Manager-Leader

As another example, my own performance type is Learner-Innovator. I have always been interested in learning about the building industry and stayed on the cutting edge of new ideas and products, especially in residential development and design. I have been insistent about using new, exciting, and well-researched home designs, materials, and colors. On the other hand, over the years I have had to employ and partner with those who had strong leadership, management, and promotional skills that insured success for my company.

As a final example, one of my business associates who manages one the largest retirement communities in the country is a Manager-Leader. He has provided an exciting and purposeful vision, strategy, and mission for his organization for many years as it grew from a family restaurant and motel into a major conference center and retirement complex of over 2000 residents. He has strengths in all five of the performance avenues, but outstanding ones in both leadership and management. He is a well-liked coach and a precise planner who insists on efficient and clearly communicated systems. He also works tirelessly with learners, innovators, and promoters to accomplish his goals and achieve long-term success. On one occasion, for example, he retained my building company to design and build an eighty-unit section of creative luxury townhouses that won a national award and sold out in only two years.

Applications

Earlier in this chapter we mentioned some of the ways performance typing can be effectively put to use in the workplace. Let's take a closer look.

Hiring. Each management position in a company should have at least two desirable performance types as part of its position description. Each candidate for the job must be evaluated to see if they fit, or come close to fitting, that performance type. A Leader-Promoter may interview very well, but if you are looking for a Manager-Innovator, this candidate needs to apply for another position. The right questions asked in writing or in an interview can determine a person's natural inclination and performance comfort zone. Don't ignore it—hire the right person for the right job.

Assignments and Promotions. The same principles for performance hiring apply to assigning employees and associates to job tasks and responsibilities and in promoting someone to a higher and often different type of position. These people have been with the company for a while and their performance types are or should be known. Why frustrate a Learner-Promoter with an innovative line management position that requires prioritizing new ventures and creating new systems? Be sure that both company management and the employee know what performance type is required for a particular assignment or promotion and try hard to make a good match—without which productivity and morale will suffer.

Team Mix. As the above meeting clearly shows, a group of different performance types create a dynamic of differing perspectives and approaches to the same challenge. This can lead to the best decision-making and problem solving if all these perspectives and approaches are analyzed and considered. Every company team does not have to have one of each performance type on it, but a healthy mix of at least several different types provides for a well-balanced team. Too many Leader-Managers and there won't be enough new and well-promoted ideas. Too many Innovator-Promoters and too little gets done on time and in budget.

Now that you have become familiar with the concept of performance typing, you are ready to discover your own performance type. The next chapter provides a test to do just that. It provides one more way—and a short and simple one at that—to find out what sort of career path is best suited for you. Should you be a CEO or on the professional staff? Should you be in research and development or in sales and marketing? Do you need to focus on ways to be more of a learner or enroll in a leadership training course? Take the test and see.

Chapter Eight

Type Testing

After a description of the five performance avenues and the ten performance types in the six previous chapters, we now turn to the Despard Performance Type Test, a testing system that allows you to discover your own performance type—that is, *knowing how you work.* Self-knowledge is a critical factor to succeeding in business. "Know thyself" the Greek philosophers emphasized (we also emphasized this in the chapter on Manager Avenue), and know it we must.

There are 20 questions and a maximum total of 100 points for each of the five performance avenues—being a leader, learner, innovator, manager or promoter. In answering each question, score yourself on a scale of one to five, *five being the highest and strongest response and one the lowest and weakest response. The mean is three, so that overall there should be as many ones as fives.*

Circle one number after each of the 20 questions and then add up your total score for each avenue. The highest score will indicate your dominant avenue, and the second highest score your secondary avenue. Put them together and you have your performance type. This system will also allow you get a sense for the performance type of others and will help you to both know and relate to them better.

There are degrees of how dominant a particular avenue is for you. You can use this information to evaluate yourself in terms of realizing your strengths and where you may need to focus attention on improving the weaker or "narrower" avenues. And remember, there are no right or wrong types and only honest and thoughtful answers will provide you with a reliable evaluation.

Leader

1. Do you consider yourself a visionary?

> 1   2   3   4   5

2. Do you often think about the direction, mission and purpose of your organization?

> 1   2   3   4   5

3. Are you a big picture kind of person?

> 1   2   3   4   5

4. Do you really like having your organization be a winner?

> 1   2   3   4   5

5. Are you willing to subordinate your own personal agenda to that of your company?

> 1   2   3   4   5

6. Have you developed a true sense of humility?

1   2   3   4   5

7. How receptive are you to taking advice and counsel from others?

1   2   3   4   5

8. Are you good at setting the right example for others to follow?

1   2   3   4   5

9. Are you an effective consensus builder?

1   2   3   4   5

10. Do you look at change as an opportunity rather than an obstacle?

1   2   3   4   5

11. Are you a strategic thinker constantly seeking a more profitable way to deploy your company's resources?

1   2   3   4   5

12. Do you have good social skills including friendliness and likeability?

1   2   3   4   5

13. Do you have a genuine empathy for others?

       1   2   3   4   5

14. Do you listen well and understand what others are communicating to you?

       1   2   3   4   5

15. Are you a good coach and teacher?

       1   2   3   4   5

16. Are you able to build synergistic teams?

       1   2   3   4   5

17. Do you have a contagious positive attitude?

       1   2   3   4   5

18. Is one of your priorities to create and maintain a fun, happy and spirited workplace?

       1   2   3   4   5

19. Do you have a passion for what you do?

       1   2   3   4   5

20. Overall, how would you rate yourself as a leader?

       1   2   3   4   5

Total *Leader* Score _____

Learner

1. Do you enjoy learning?

     1   2   3   4   5

2. Are you inspired and energized by it?

     1   2   3   4   5

3. Are you a curious person who likes digging into facts, figures and details?

     1   2   3   4   5

4. How observant are you?

     1   2   3   4   5

5. Do you do a lot of learning such as reading, asking questions, listening to others, getting out into the field or onto plant floor and attending conferences and seminars?

     1   2   3   4   5

6. How important is learning to gaining understanding and wisdom?

     1   2   3   4   5

7. How crucial is knowledge to reducing the risk of making mistakes?

     1   2   3   4   5

8. Do you think that the greater your knowledge of the arts and sciences, the better you can perform your job?

1   2   3   4   5

9. To what extent do you believe that knowledge can change and even transform people?

1   2   3   4   5

10. Are you a researcher who likes to do his homework?

1   2   3   4   5

11. Do you like to look at many alternatives before making a decision?

1   2   3   4   5

12. How important is it to understand right- or left-brain dominance, personality types, management styles and performance types?

1   2   3   4   5

13. Are you good at benchmarking the best practices in your industry?

1   2   3   4   5

14. How well do you learn from your customers?

1   2   3   4   5

15. How well do you learn from your competition?

      1   2   3   4   5

16. How well do you learn from both your successful experiences and your mistakes?

      1   2   3   4   5

17. Do you strive to provide an educational and training environment within your company as well as learning experiences outside of your company?

      1   2   3   4   5

18. To what extent must today's workers be proactive learners in order to succeed?

      1   2   3   4   5

19. Are you always seeking new ways to apply what you have learned?

      1   2   3   4   5

20. Overall, how would you rate yourself as a learner?

      1   2   3   4   5

Total *Learner* Score _____

Innovator

1. How creative are you?

        1   2   3   4   5

2. Are you eager to express that creativity in ways that will improve your business?

        1   2   3   4   5

3. Are you a dreamer who imagines what could be?

        1   2   3   4   5

4. Do you like to experiment with things that might lead to a new invention or product?

        1   2   3   4   5

5. Do you agree with the concept that bright ideas are not an accident?

        1   2   3   4   5

6. Do you eagerly assist in the creation of and/or embrace paradigm shifts in your company or industry?

        1   2   3   4   5

7. Are you energized by "engaging the chaos"—that is, the confusion associated with change?

        1   2   3   4   5

8. Are you constantly seeking new opportunities and business ventures?

1   2   3   4   5

9. Do you strive to beat the competition by innovating?

1   2   3   4   5

10. Do you have a strong positive can-do attitude with regard to innovations?

1   2   3   4   5

11. Are you temporarily satisfied when you have created several innovations or do you keep looking for more?

1   2   3   4   5

12. Do you focus a lot of thought and energy on how to transform your business through innovative changes?

1   2   3   4   5

13. Do you like to brainstorm for new ideas with your associates?

1   2   3   4   5

14. Are you good at taking an old idea and putting it to new uses?

1   2   3   4   5

15. Do you often take successful ideas from another industry and applying it to your business?

1   2   3   4   5

16. Are you willing to take the risk of trying something new and unknown?

1   2   3   4   5

17. Are you persistent and not bothered by experiments that fail at first?

1   2   3   4   5

18. Do multiple things motivate you to innovate such as creative satisfaction, meeting an exciting challenge, and making a profit from it?

1   2   3   4   5

19. How important is it to differentiate your company and its products?

1   2   3   4   5

20. Overall, how would you rate yourself as an innovator?

1   2   3   4   5

Total *Innovator* Score _____

Manager

1. Do you like to set goals and objectives for yourself and your company?

1   2   3   4   5

2. Are you well organized and do you prefer a predictable, structured work environment?

1   2   3   4   5

3. Do you look forward to, and are you effective at, projecting and budgeting?

1   2   3   4   5

4. To what extent do you believe there is a management system for everything?

1   2   3   4   5

5. Are you good at prioritizing—that is, putting first things first?

1   2   3   4   5

6. Do you get things done in a timely manner without procrastinating?

1   2   3   4   5

7. Do you have a high degree of emotional intelligence?

1   2   3   4   5

8. Do you delegate well?

1   2   3   4   5

9. Is one of your strengths recruiting people that are smarter than you are?

1   2   3   4   5

10. Are you an effective decision maker and problem solver?

1   2   3   4   5

12. Do you communicate and interact well with other people?

1   2   3   4   5

12. How important is it to build trusting relationships with your associates?

1   2   3   4   5

13. Are you effective at empowering others to do their jobs well?

1   2   3   4   5

14. Do you respect your associates and treat them as partners?

1   2   3   4   5

15. Do you to admit your mistakes quickly and emphatically?

        1   2   3   4   5

16. Is "efficiency" your middle name?

        1   2   3   4   5

17. Are you a practical results oriented person?

        1   2   3   4   5

18. Are you good at maintaining control in any situation?

        1   2   3   4   5

19. Do you take a direct and objective approach to management?

        1   2   3   4   5

20. Overall, how do you rate yourself as a manager?

        1   2   3   4   5

Total *Manager* Score _____

Promoter

1. Do you have an outgoing friendly personality?

    1   2   3   4   5

2. How strongly believe in the concept that perception is everything?

    1   2   3   4   5

3. Do you make enthusiastic presentations?

    1   2   3   4   5

4. Are you a persuasive person?

    1   2   3   4   5

5. Are you a skillful win/win negotiator?

    1   2   3   4   5

6. How aware are you that you are nearly always promoting something or someone—such as an approach, a concept, an idea, a proposal, a service, a product or a person?

    1   2   3   4   5

7. Do you enjoy, and are you successful at, one-on-one selling?

    1   2   3   4   5

8. Do you always make a first good impression when meeting someone?

1   2   3   4   5

9. Do you normally look at the bright side of things?

1   2   3   4   5

10. How well do you comply with the notion that selling is a series of getting to one "yes" at a time?

1   2   3   4   5

11. How observant and sensitive are you to others' words, tone of voice, body language and facial expressions in their response to you as a promoter?

1   2   3   4   5

12. To what extent is the messenger the message?

1   2   3   4   5

13. Are you an exciting storyteller?

1   2   3   4   5

14. Are you an actor with a sense of drama?

1   2   3   4   5

15. Are you a winning evangelist for your cause?

1   2   3   4   5

16. Are you an effective and popular politician?

1   2   3   4   5

17. To what extent do you insist on selling things rather than have them sell themselves?

1   2   3   4   5

18. How persistent are you, particularly in view of failed promotional activities?

1   2   3   4   5

19. Are sales managers, advertising people and marketing directors your favorite kinds of people?

1   2   3   4   5

20. Overall, how would you rate yourself as a promoter?

1   2   3   4   5

Total *Promoter* Score _____

Summary

Leader Score _____

Learner Score _____

Innovator Score _____

Manager Score _____

Promoter Score _____

Note: If two or more of your highest scores are within three points of each other, you may want to actually select another dominant and/or secondary performance avenue by asking yourself further related questions and by reviewing the behavioral traits of each of the five avenues found in Chapters Two through Six. It may also help to review your answers to some or all of the questions to be sure you answered them as accurately as possible. *List the secondary avenue first using it in a sense as an adjective for your most dominant avenue.* For example, what kind of leader are you? An Innovator-Leader. What kind of promoter are you? A Learner-Promoter.

Dominant Performance Avenue:

_____

Secondary Performance Avenue:

_____

Performance Type:

_____

Chapter Nine

Balancing and Blending

We have discussed the five modes of operation we use every day in all that we do. You have had a chance to study and understand these five performance avenues and determine your own performance type. We are now ready to see how they relate to one another in terms of their *quantity* or *degree*—too much of one and not enough of another—that we call *balancing*. And then to see them in terms of their level of *quality* and how well they interact with one another, that we call *blending*. For example, if you are an innovator who likes to promote, being aware of the need for you to increase the intensity of your leading, learning, and managing (balancing) and looking for ways take advantage of everyone's stronger avenues (blending) will elevate you and your company to a higher level of performance.

We all have latent gifts and talents that can be crowded out by even greater gifts and talents. It is important to establish a point of activity below which no avenue can go and realize that overly dominant avenues must be moderated and held in check—in other words, to balance your performance avenues within reasonable limits. We will do that under the section entitled "Balancing Your Avenues."

We all tend to think we can perform well on all five avenues only to lose the advantages gained by combining our own strengths as well as the strengths of other team members. Under a second section entitled "Blending Your Avenues," we will discuss *merging* avenues and how best to relate one avenue to another so that the sum of the parts, both individually and corporately, is far better than any one part. This *synergy* is the essence of improving both your performance and that of the team.

Both balancing and blending your capabilities and your approach to operating your business will take varying amounts of time and effort depending on where you start. *But we all start somewhere and it's taking the right road that counts.*

Balancing Your Avenues

Your Dominant Avenue. There is a similar heading in Chapter One, Reading Your Map that encourages the reader to determine his or her dominant avenue. Now that you have visualized yourself as primarily a leader, learner, innovator, manager, or promoter, let's see if your initial impressions are correct and how to make any necessary adjustments to allow your secondary avenues to come into greater play.

It's fine to have one dominant avenue—in fact, we all have one—but it's not fine to have a domineering avenue. A domineering avenue takes charge at the expense of the other avenues and stands alone. If, for example, you are a super promoter and go about promoting without sufficient learning and managing, you end up being a disorganized salesperson who doesn't know what they are talking about. Ever met one of those people? That's not you at times, is it?

If you find yourself on a domineering avenue, simply slow down and pull off to the side of the road. Then look at the map and drive on another avenue for a while. For example, if you are an unappreciated innovator, a little time on Promoter Avenue will help you better promote your ideas to your associates and to the marketplace.

Your Secondary Avenue. Everybody has a secondary avenue too. And determining and understanding this avenue is the beginning of a more balanced approach to your personal and professional decision-making and behavior. It's the main support for your dominant avenue and keeps it from becoming domineering one. Perhaps the most effective secondary avenue for an innovator is being a learner so that that you have more knowledge to innovate with. A leader backed up by promotional skills can better sell a company's vision, mission, and strategy.

You can see where we are headed. We are now allowing lesser avenues to intensify and become more equal to the others. But if two avenues become a domineering combination, we are back to the same problem. You need to drive on all of your performance avenues for a minimum amount of time in order to keep things in balance.

Driving on the Narrower Avenues. Once you have identified your dominant and secondary avenues, you are ready to check the strength of the three remaining ones. You may have more knowledge and skills on the narrower avenues than you realize.

There are reasons why you drive on them less. It has to do with your personality type, thinking style, emotional intelligence, and comfort zone. You may, for example, be a great leader with backup management ability, but are not particularly interested in learning and innovating, which results in your being less of a leader. *Do not live in denial* that there is an avenue-balancing problem—define the problem and then go about solving it.

Pick an avenue that you realize is narrow—it may be restricted or blocked in some way. Think through what some of the causes might be, come up with some suggestions on how to improve your performance on these avenues and prioritize actions to correct the situation. Read an article or book, go to a seminar and seek the advice and counsel of others who can help you. You may need training in leadership, management or sales. And don't rule out psychological evaluations, profiling or testing of some kind.

Remember that change is usually slow and painful, but is well worth all the effort. Sometimes very simple changes can make a big difference in a particular area. Other times, it takes much longer and you seem to get nowhere. It helps to set some goals for minimum standards in each of the five avenues so you can monitor your own performance. For example, if you want to be more of an innovator, set a goal of dreaming up one great new idea a month for your company. That way you will start to focus more on innovation.

So be sure none of your avenues are domineering, complement your dominant avenue with your secondary avenue and increase the activity of your narrower avenues. It's a balancing act that provides stability and consistency to you as a performer.

Corporate Balancing. Problems in companies can occur when they have, for example, too many leaders and innovators and not enough learners, managers, and promoters. Stop, define the problem and re-balance the team with a better ratio of team members who have different dominant performance avenues. It is not a matter of having 20% of each, but of knowing who's who and having an appropriate and workable mix to accomplish the task assigned to each team.

Our firm, Despard Associates, LLC, does consulting work with other builders and developers. One of our clients was an executive with a large manufacturing company for many years in various capacities and locations. He reviewed an early manuscript of this book and related the situation he found at his company regarding the performance avenues of their executives.

In looking back he now realizes that most of the executives were promoters who were very good at promoting themselves and their own ideas that made them both appear as good as possible. That approach represented the corporate performance culture. This executive is a highly efficient manger who progressed up through the ranks and had an impressive career with the company. In the wisdom of hindsight, he believes that if he had paid more attention to his promotional side, he would have advanced even faster and farther. He admits that he usually assumed that his ideas would sell themselves. I experienced the same thing as a homebuilder in thinking that my new model homes were of such superior design and quality that they would sell themselves, but soon learned that an added appeal of exciting marketing helped sell them more quickly and at a better price.

Companies often have too many of their executives who are most natural and comfortable on the same performance avenue at the expense of the other four. Diversity of performance avenues within an organization is the key to a well-balanced team. That's why dominant performance avenue evaluations need to be incorporated into hiring, training, and promoting practices. This performance balancing helps make a company a dynamic one that is ready, willing, and able to assertively face challenges and deal effectively with change.

Blending Your Avenues

Merging. Now that we have balanced the traffic and have a closer vehicle count on each avenue, imagine five lanes merging into one. Initially, traffic backs up and there is chaos and road rage, but eventually it flows smoothly again. Merging our performance avenues is like that—there is going to be some upheaval before things settle down. But as we mentioned in the chapter on Innovator Avenue, we have to engage a certain amount of chaos to get to the next level of performance.

Merging is the catalyst that helps the performance avenues communicate and work together. It takes advantage of where the avenues are complementary and overlap, defines their distinctiveness, and highlights their effectiveness.

There is both individual and corporate merging. An example of individual merging is allowing your learning skills to enhance your ability to lead by not just the quantity of learning, but the focused and practical quality of it as it relates to leadership. Determine what a leader needs to know and search for that knowledge. Learning about being a visionary, consensus building and socializing helps improve your performance as a leader.

An example of corporate merging is the need for your company to grow its profits by developing a new product. First, leadership is needed to provide the vision and mission that is followed by learning for the research, innovation for the product idea, management to get it produced efficiently, and promotion to market and sell it. *This is an example of a start-to-finish chain of events and a chain is only as strong as its weakest link.*

Synergy. While you have to be a juggler and keep five balls in the air at one time, your performance on all five avenues will not be the same. If you are a born salesperson, you will always do exceptionally well on Promoter Avenue. But you do have to juggle the other four balls to please the crowd in order to have a successful, seamless performance.

You do not, however, have to be a hero and to be all things to all people. That's where teamwork and using the whole brain of the company comes into play. You need to understand your own strengths as well as the strengths of others on your team. If you are not a good manager, find others who are and let them do more work where management skills are required. With effective synergy, the sum of the parts is better than any of the individual parts.

The final goal of balancing and blending our individual and corporate performance avenues is a grand avenue that combines the best of each avenue and results in the peak performance of both you and your company. In the next and final chapter we will look at how to use the self- knowledge of your performance type to reach and stay on top of your game—that is, to operate at peak performance.

Chapter Ten

Performance Peak

The Grand Teton Range of the Rocky Mountains in Wyoming has many high and majestic peaks. On one expedition in this range, our band of explorers consisting of a group of hometown friends, kept trying to hike to one higher peak after another. It took a map, some planning, a compass, and lots of effort and perseverance. We were not satisfied until we reached the highest peak that was possible with our skills, knowledge, and equipment.

In business, there is always a higher peak of some kind to be climbed. It may simply be doing what we do better or a paradigm shift to a new venture. In the last chapter of this book we are providing a summary discussion of how get to and stay at your highest possible Performance Peak by offering the following four sections—*Getting There, Staying There, Your Health,* and *Your Purpose.*

Getting There

Your career is an interesting and long journey with many peaks and valleys, side roads, and stops along the way. You are already at a peak of some kind since have achieved a measure of success in your field of endeavor. You know how high it is, how hard it was to get there, and whether or not you are ready, willing, and able to go the next peak.

We will now look at getting to that next peak by establishing a *starting point*, reviewing the *strengths and weaknesses of your performance type*, setting some *goals and objectives for a higher peak performance,* and formulating an *individual action plan.*

Starting Point. Do a hard and honest appraisal of your current level of performance. You probably have a pretty good idea of where you stand, but need to give it a little more thought, particularly in view of reading this book. Check the degree of your satisfaction with your own job performance—the less satisfied you are, the farther you have to go to your own performance peak.

Then try an informal comparative analysis with other businessmen and women beginning with your head-to-head competitors and going to other contemporaries in your industry as well as those in other industries. What are their approaches to their businesses and how well are they running them? See where you stack up and establish your starting point.

Strengths and Weaknesses of Your Performance Type. As you saw from the analysis of the ten performance types, every type has its own strengths and weaknesses. After selecting your type and studying its *Passing Lanes, Detours* and *Are likely to* sections, expand the list with further strengths and weaknesses that specifically apply to you. You will then have a complete description of yourself as a business performer.

You know what needs attention and what doesn't. For example, you may have determined that you need to learn more by delving deeper into things and that some sales training would help your promotional activities. Or that you are a good leader, but a more consistent flow of bright ideas would make you a more effective one.

You may remember from Chapter Five, Manager Avenue that the first step in solving a problem is defining it. After defining your performance type and level of performance, you can proceed to set some goals and find ways to improve your performance.

Goals and Objectives for a Higher Performance Peak. Put your manager's hat on and set some realistic performance goals for the next 12 to 18 months. After determining how high a peak you want to shoot for, take each of the five avenues and challenge yourself accordingly. For example, as a leader you want to do more consensus building, as a learner more benchmarking, as an innovator more coming up with bright ideas, as a manager more systematizing, as a promoter more persuasive negotiating, and so on. Set some targets, quantify them, and write them down.

Back up each goal with some specific objectives such as more team meetings for consensus building, more research on your competitors for benchmarking, more long-term big picture thinking for creating a paradigm, more time spent on devising systems for systematizing, and paying more attention to win/win solutions for persuasive negotiating. Get the picture? It's not that hard once you get started.

Individual Action Plan. Basically, planning is organizing, prioritizing, and providing structure to your goals and objectives with ways to carry them out as well as establishing both a timeline and time in your schedule to get the job done. In continuing to develop the above examples, part of an individual action plan would be having team meetings every two weeks, spending one day per month studying your competition, scheduling some specific times and places to reflect more and write down your thoughts, working with a consultant on more efficient management systems, and role playing to practice your selling and negotiating skills. An individual action plan is similar to and works in tandem with a company's business plan and needs to be measured, monitored, and modified. It adds a lot of value to you and your performance. *Make it a habit to develop a road map for going to your next highest Performance Peak.*

Staying There

"Staying there" simply means staying on top of your game. That may mean maintaining and improving an already high level of performance and being sure you do not backslide and lose altitude, or as we described above, preparing yourself for the next highest attainable peak. *The Performance Peak goal is to be always driving in high gear whether you have reached your peak performance or not.*

The first thing is to hold on to your current level of performance. It is not hard to become complacent and slip little by little over time. That's why all the evaluating and appraising we have talked about in this book is so important. As we mentioned in the chapter on managing, good companies can go bad—so can good people. We cannot stand still any more than the fast-changing world around us does.

Here is a checklist list of things business performers need to think about in order to stay on top and keep their organizations on top with them.

Performance Punch List

- Gain a working knowledge of the five performance avenues.
- Determine your performance type.

- Know your current level of performance and how much it can be improved.
- Develop a system to be sure you are not back-sliding or losing altitude.
- Set some goals and objectives for your current and future Performance Peaks.
- Have an Individual Action Plan—your road map—in place at all times.
- Continually learn, create, innovate and persevere.
- Examine the relationship between your performance and that of your organization—are they at the same level and going in the same direction?
- Lead, manage, and promote your company in attaining its highest peak performance in the same way you do that for yourself.

Striving to get and stay at Performance Peak for you and your business feeds on itself—it is an exciting exercise that continually energizes you and keeps you mentally and emotionally fit. You have read this book, given it some thought and come up with some sort of action plan. Keep it handy in the future and use it as a reference guide from time to time.

Before we conclude there are two additional areas of your life that are critical to attaining and maintaining your peak performance—your health and your purpose, that we will briefly examine next.

Your Health

If you are in perfect physical and mental health, have no bad habits, exercise regularly and eat well, go on to the next section now. If not, take a few minutes to evaluate your health and realize its importance to achieving a high level of performance in all that you do.

Your performance in business is affected by your mental and physical health—perhaps more than we understand. Emotional problems involving unresolved anger or your self-image, for example, can seriously lower your performance without you even knowing it—sometimes we live in denial and don't want to know it. So make sure you are in good mental health if you expect to reach your peak performance.

Our physical health is equally important since our minds and bodies are so closely connected and interdependent. Act on good advice about exercise and nutrition. For example, our consumption of refined sugar (an average of 150 pounds per year), alcohol and caffeine can cause chemical imbalances in our bodies that lead to mineral depletion, enzyme and organ malfunction, indigestion, irritability and, over time, the degradation of the immune system.

With regard to stress, a measure of it is healthy, but too much of it will adversely affect your performance through fatigue and burnout. Worse, when stress becomes *distress*, the obstacles to success become even greater. *Don't try to change your lifestyle overnight, but make a commitment to improve it steadily.*

Your Purpose

Is it philosophically possible to have performance without purpose? My answer is clearly no, but it is a deep question for each reader to consider. In striving towards success and achievement, we tend to dwell on its immediate purpose of earning a living and having the material things of life.

But the higher the performance, the greater the need to seek life's meaning and purpose. The more we look at ultimate reality and our reason for being, the more convicted and committed we will be to doing our best everyday. It is our responsibility to find and use our gifts and talents to the fullest. All work has dignity and worth and is performed for a purpose.

The logo of the YMCA is a triangle with the words mind, body, and spirit. It means that there are three interrelated parts of a person and each must be well for the whole person to be well. *Continue to do some serious soul searching and connect your spiritual life to your actions so that your personal and professional performance becomes based on your purpose in life.*

A Final Stop

In concluding this book, let's highlight what it means to be a *dynamic* performer. Webster's Unabridged Second Edition of its *New Twentieth Century Dictionary* defines dynamic in part, as "involving or causing energy, motion, action or change, as opposed to being static; vigorous and forceful." *And so a dynamic business performance is full of energy, vitality, action, and change.* It is a performance that is constantly in motion and both prepared and eager to embrace change, change that transforms us.

There are five avenues that we perform on in all areas of our lives. Though some are more dominant than others, they are all important avenues to our success and ultimately to our peak performance.

By determining and understanding our performance type, we understand ourselves better and understand and work with others better. By improving our performance on each avenue, we improve our total performance. By balancing and blending them, we have a dynamic individual and company performance.

Appendix

Outline of the Five Performance Avenues

Leader Avenue

Vision, direction and purpose. Being a visionary.
Corporate Climate—Subordination, humility, expectations and examples, fact versus fiction, the whole brain of a company, consensus building and change.
Conversion and new converts.
Futuring—Strategic thinking, seeking new challenges, differentiation and realistic forecasting.
Socializing—Limited friendship, likeability and empathy.
Coaching—Listening, teaching, criticizing, team building, mediating and passion.
Benefitting—Organizational spirit; personal compensation.

Learner Avenue

The Learning Ladder: Phase I—Data, history, information and knowledge; Phase II—Understanding, practical intelligence, wisdom and conviction; Phase III—Influencing, change and transformation.

Smart choices, alternatives and decision-making.

Learning by researching, understanding people, benchmarking and learning from your customers, competition and mistakes.

Innovator Avenue

Innovation is practical applied creativity.

The Art of Innovation—Dream machine, paradigms, bright ideas, engaging the chaos and entrepreneurship.

The Results of Innovation—Profitability, competitive advantage, business growth, long-term success and energized and excited employees, associates and customers.

Innovate with attitude, thinking, practice, brainstorming, imitation, niches, and risk.

Manager Avenue

Planning—Interpreting and translating the strategy, goals and objectives, budgeting, organizing and prioritizing and communicating, monitoring and adjusting the plan.

Systematizing –Shared creation of systems, delegating and checks and balances.

Directing—Decision-making, problem solving, interacting, empowerment and getting outcomes-based results.

All managers need preparation, drive and alliances.

Manager's Field Guide—Know thyself, do not live in denial, communicate and understand, be objective, admit your mistakes, build relationships, etc.

Promoter Avenue

Promotion is perception, presentation and persuasion.

Win/win negotiating.

Who to sell to, client partnering and the reasons to promote yourself and your business.

The Message—Total sales and marketing package, memorable message, trust, integrity and reliability and the customer's experience with your company.

The Messenger—The messenger is the message; storyteller, evangelist and politician.

The Reply—Analyzing and responding to customer feedback to your promotions and your products and services.

References and Suggested Reading

Benfari, Robert, *Understanding and Changing Your Management Style*, San Francisco: Jossey-Bass Inc., 1999

Covey, Stephen, *The Seven Habits of Highly Effective People*, New York: Simon & Schuster, 1989

Dell, Michael, *Direct From Dell*, New York: HarperCollins Publishers, Inc., 1999

Despard, Thomas, *The Strategic Thinking Process for Home Builders*, Washington: National Association of Home Builders, 2000

Despard, Thomas, *The Business Planning Process for Home Builders*, Washington: National Association of Home Builders, 2000

Drucker, Peter, *Innovation and Entrepreneurship*, New York: HarperCollins Publishers, Inc., 1985

Fisher, Roger and William Ury, *Getting to Yes*, New York: Penguin Books USA, Inc., 2nd Edition, 1991

Gelb, Michael, *How to Think Like Leonardo da Vinci*, New York: Random House, Inc., 1998

Goleman, Daniel, *Working with Emotional Intelligence*, New York: Bantam Books, 1998

Hammond, John, Ralph Keeney and Howard Raiffa, *Smart Choices*, Boston: Harvard Business School Press, 1999

Harvard Business Review, *On Knowledge Management*, Boston: Harvard Business School Press, 1998

Katzenbach, Jon, *Peak Performance*, Boston: Harvard Business School Press, 2000

Kriegel, Robert and Louis Patler, *If it ain't broke...BREAK IT!*, New York: Warner Books, Inc., 1991

Kummerow, Jean, Nancy Barger and Linda Kirby, *Work Types*, New York: Warner Books, Inc., 1997

Pine, Joseph and James Gilmore, *The Experience Economy*, Boston: Harvard Business School Press, 1999

Trout, Jack, *The Power of Simplicity*, New York: McGraw-Hill Companies, Inc., 1999

Vance, Mike and Diane Deacon, *RAISE THE BAR*, Franklin Lakes, NJ: Career Press, Inc., 1999

Wheeler, Jim, *The Power of Innovative Thinking*, Franklin Lakes, NJ: Career Press, Inc., 1998

Wilson, Larry, *Stop Selling, Start Partnering*, New York: John Wiley & Sons, Inc., 1994

About the Author

Tom Despard is a graduate of Vanderbilt University and has been an engineer, a general contractor, a homebuilder, a developer, an author and a businessman in Pennsylvania for over 30 years. He was a partner and executive in one construction firm and the CEO and owner of another one. He is currently President of Despard Associates, LLC and a Realtor and consultant with Commercial Prime Properties, both of Lancaster, PA.

His business books include *The Strategic Thinking Process for Home Builders* and *The Business Planning Process for Home Builders* both published by the National Association of Home Builders, Washington, DC, *Performance Avenues, Knowing How We Work* published by Xulon Press, Fairfax, VA and *The V-Link, Connecting Virtues and Vocations*.

CPSIA information can be obtained at www.ICGtesting.com
Printed in the USA
267130BV00001B/32/A

9 781931 232982